Heritage Trees
of
Scotland

Heritage Trees
of
Scotland

Donald Rodger, Jon Stokes and James Ogilvie
Photographs by Archie Miles and Edward Parker

Edited by Charlton Clark

Foreword by The Duke of Buccleuch, KT

Published by Forestry Commission Scotland
in association with the Tree Council

Heritage Trees of Scotland

Authors   Donald Rodger (Arboricultural Consultant), Jon Stokes
                     (Tree Council) and James Ogilvie (Forestry Commission Scotland)
Editor   Charlton Clark (Forestry Commission)
Art Director   Archie Miles
Photography   Archie Miles and Edward Parker

First published in Great Britain in 2006 by:

Forestry Commission Scotland,

Silvan House, 231 Corstorphine Road, Edinburgh EH12 7AT

and The Tree Council,

71 Newcomen Street, London SE1 1YT

Designed by Carter Graphics, Worcester
Image scanning by Greenshires Group Ltd, Leicester
Printing and Binding by Tien Wah Press Pte Ltd

A CIP catalogue record for this book is available from the British Library.

ISBN 0-904853-06-3

Cover photograph: The Coventanters' Oak, Archie Miles

Papers used in the production of this book are made from wood pulp originating from sustainably managed
plantations. Wherever possible, woodland waste such as tree tops, trimmings, sawdust and wood shavings are
used. The paper is chlorine free, acid free, recyclable and bio-degradable.

Contents

Heritage Trees
of
Scotland

NATIONAL
DISTRIBUTION MAP

Regional Maps

Bowhill, Selkirk, Scotland

Foreword

By the Duke of Buccleuch, KT

In these days when climate change threatens to change so much of our lives, the life-enhancing virtue of trees is slowly becoming more widely appreciated. Yet because their lifespan can be many times that of man's, we still tend to regard them as permanent features to be taken for granted. However, if we just try to imagine the towns and cities without their parks, squares and tree-lined streets, or our rural landscape devoid of their most significant features, our appreciation of them is immediately sharpened. No matter whether they appear singly as humble hedgerow trees or avenues, in clumps and spinneys, as shelterbelts or in great forests, they are there to refresh the soul of man and physically purify the air we breathe.

This very welcome second edition of Heritage Trees of Scotland comes at a time when "short-termism" is taking over the long-term planning of our forebears, as exemplified by my favourites in this fascinating selection, the many venerable trees of great age. So much of our wonderful landscape and all within it, which we so greatly value today, is the direct result of the forethought of those living three or four hundred years ago. What an example this is for us to plan for future generations! Even the Fortingall Yew in Perthshire, still living and possibly already 3000 years old at the first Christmas, might be credited to one of our ancestors.

Introduction

The Balmerino Sweet Chestnut

What is a heritage tree?

If the world of trees can be likened to the world of people, then heritage trees are the "characters". They're exceptional, extraordinary, uncommon and unexpected. Often they inspire wonder and awe; sometimes they instil humility and modesty; always they capture one's imagination. You might be surprised or even amazed by a heritage tree, but you'll never be indifferent. Such trees play a vital and defining part in a country's natural and cultural heritage, particularly in Scotland, which boasts probably the richest legacy of heritage trees in the world.

These national arboricultural treasures are living milestones, and although you won't find a scientific definition in your dictionary of arboriculture, there is no doubting that, once observed, a heritage tree is at once a distinctive and recognisable character. Be it a lofty sentinel in the landscape or a wizened courtyard guardian, a single botanical curiosity or a sacred grove of veterans, a heritage tree has an appeal beyond time and space. Such trees afford us mere mortals a brief glimpse of immortality, providing a living timeline back through the centuries and a physical presence greater than our own small, earthly stature. Thanks to Scotland's colourful history, its rich culture and its benign growing conditions, this nation has proved to be a fertile

environment where heritage trees have grown and
flourished. Whatever form they take and wherever
they happen to be, such trees are a priceless
resource for Scotland: heirlooms of the nation, to
be treasured and nurtured by this generation, then
handed on to the next to steward, appreciate,
admire and cherish.

What are the characteristics of heritage trees?

Although there is no single definition of
heritage trees, they can be grouped into different
categories. Some belong to one category, whilst
others may belong to several. Many heritage trees

Arran whitebeam.

are ancient specimens: veteran survivors of a bygone age. Some are champions and
giants, having record dimensions such as tallest, widest or largest. Some are trees with a
uniquely Scottish connection, important historically or culturally. Several are weird and
wonderful, having an unusual or grotesque appearance. A few are botanical curiosities:
introductions and rarities that form a living legacy of Scotland's plant hunters and
collectors, or particular rarities with a special botanical interest. And then there are the
named individuals and groups of trees: singletons, avenues and groves of particular
importance or significance.

What kinds of heritage tree are there?

Ancient trees of great age for their species (veterans) can typically range from 200
years old in the case of "short-lived" species such as birch, to 1000 years and more for
long-lived species such as yew. It is exceptional age for the species concerned which
warrants the term heritage, not simply old age in itself. For example, oaks such as the
Cadzow group can live for centuries, some being as old as our medieval cathedrals.
The Lochwood Oaks, for example, allowed dendrochronologists to construct a tree-ring
sequence stretching back to 1571. However, it is the yews which really stretch the
imagination, living as they can for several thousand years. Indeed, the oldest tree in
Europe, the remarkable Fortingall Yew, is reckoned to be up to 5,000 years old, which,
if true, would make it as old as Stonehenge.

Exceptionally large specimens (champions and giants) abound in Scotland. These trees are invariably impressive specimens of their species, representing the ultimate in height or girth so far achieved (most of them are still growing taller). The 19th century North American introductions enjoy Scotland's mild, wet climate, producing an array of huge conifers. These include the United Kingdom's tallest tree (a distinction disputed by the Douglas firs at Reelig Glen and the Hermitage); the largest-girthed tree – a giant redwood at Cluny Garden; and The Mightiest Conifer in Europe at Ardkinglas Woodland Garden on the shores of Loch Fyne. Broadleaves can also reach epic proportions in Scotland, such as the largest-girthed sweet chestnut, at Cockairnie near Aberdour, or the world-beating beech hedge at Meikleour.

Trees with historical and cultural connections (uniquely Scottish) play a prominent and much-loved part in the country's cultural heritage. Many of these trees are associated with important and colourful events or people in Scotland's past. Others have been planted to commemorate a particular occasion. These uniquely Scottish trees act as

Cadzow Oaks in medieval wood pasture in South Lanarkshire.

a living link with the nation's history, and include the Wallace Yew, Queen Mary's Thorn and the Covenanters' Oak.

Trees of unusual growth habit, strange appearance and character (weird and wonderful) can either be naturally strange or made freakish by human intervention. Trees displaying unusual or

One of many Corstorphine sycamores to be found around Edinburgh.

atypical growth habits often create botanically interesting and visually striking objects: unique wonders of the arboricultural world. These include such oddities as the weeping larch at Kelburn, the "pedestal" larch at Dunkeld House, the Twin Trees of Finzean, and a handful of great "layering" yews, such as Ormiston and Whittingehame. Trees made unnatural by human intervention include the Bicycle Tree at Brig o' Turk and the Wishing Tree in Argyll.

Botanically significant trees (introductions and rarities) exist in diverse corners of Scotland. For example, Scotland contains native species not found naturally elsewhere, such as the two whitebeam species found only on the island of Arran. There are also botanical mutants, comprising unique genotypes, such as Scotland's original progenitors of the fastigiate beech at Dawyck, the Camperdown Elm near Dundee, and the Corstorphine Sycamore in Edinburgh. Other heritage trees, often held in collections, include the earliest introductions by Scotland's famous plant collectors such as David Douglas (the Douglas fir at Scone), Henry Veitch (the Japanese larches at Dunkeld) and James Naesmyth (the European larch at Dawyck and Kailzie).

Celebrity trees, avenues and groves (named individuals and groups) are usually well-known local features, often appearing as named trees on old maps. They are often associated with some historical event, and are invariably local landmarks of strong community significance. Examples include the Capon Tree near Jedburgh, Queen Mary's Thorn at St Andrews, and the Wallace Yew in Renfrewshire. Others might occur in avenues and groves, forming valuable landscape features in their own right. The Act of Union Beeches at North Berwick, the mighty Redwood Avenue at Benmore, and Diana's Grove at Blair Castle are three notable examples.

The Birnam Sycamore – just one of Big Tree Country's splendid specimens.

Where are heritage trees of Scotland to be found?

They exist throughout the length and breadth of Scotland, from the Northern Isles to the Scottish Borders, and from Aberdeenshire to Moidart. They can crop up in the most unlikely places (the grounds of an ordnance factory, for example, or the wilds of an Argyll moor, or even in suburban gardens), but in practice most are found on landed estates and in formal gardens and tree collections. In particular, Scotland's owners of large landholdings have a long and illustrious history of tree collecting and planting, often stretching back for many generations. Many important heritage trees are found within the grounds of such estates, most of which are open to the public. Heritage trees also occur in public parks, open spaces and land owned or managed by organisations such as Forestry Commission Scotland, National Trust for Scotland and Historic Scotland.

Perthshire ("Big Tree Country") is arguably the epicentre of Scotland's heritage trees. It boasts Europe's oldest tree, the world's highest hedge, a rival to Britain's tallest tree, and a plethora of other notables. No fewer than seven heritage trees can be found close to Dunkeld. Other concentrations can be found in parts of Argyll and the Central Belt.

Why are heritage trees important?

Heritage trees are priceless. They are unique and irreplaceable living organisms with a value which cannot meaningfully be measured in any currency. Collectively, their value to botanical understanding, to tree improvement, as landscape features, as habitats for wildlife, and in historic and cultural terms is immense. Some are as important as Scotland's stately homes and castles, yet, remarkably, there is no special protection for trees of such significance. Tree Preservation Orders offer some

Sitka spruce at Fairburn House in Easter Ross.

legal protection, but a heritage tree covered by a TPO is the exception rather than the rule. The fact that Scotland still contains arguably the richest resource of heritage trees in the world has been due more to good fortune than good design. Indeed, until recently, most of Scotland's great trees had been overlooked, taken largely for granted by the few folk who knew about them. Little was known about their whereabouts, and even less about their condition. Many were sorely neglected and at risk, while others were gradually becoming lost through ignorance, neglect, apathy and vandalism. This tragic loss continues even today. Only recently, some notable heritage trees have been lost through ignorance and greed (see In Memoriam on page 22).

Are heritage trees safe?

Although many heritage trees have existed in harmony with their environment for centuries, they are particularly vulnerable to the damaging impacts of human activity. An ancient tree which might have borne silent witness to significant events in Scotland's history can be felled in a matter of minutes and

The Gordon Castle holly. This massive old coppiced holly was photographed by Elwes & Henry in 1906. There is now no trace of it – a heritage tree lost.

destroyed within a matter of hours. Like old people, old trees can be particularly vulnerable. Wonderful veterans continue to be lost every year. Combined with the misuse of technology, ignorance is the greatest threat of all.

Threats appear in a variety of guises, from overt human pressures such as urban development, vandalism, damaging maintenance, people pressure and rural development, to more subtle agents such as pests and diseases, to future changes as yet unknown – pollution and climate change, for example.

What are the threats to heritage trees?

Urban development – An ever-increasing demand for buildings and associated infrastructure constitutes possibly the greatest threat to heritage trees in Scotland. The value of land for housing and retail development puts any tree occupying the same space at great risk. Even if it remains standing, the damage from cable and pipe trenches, spoil dumping or soil compaction can effectively seal the tree's death warrant long after the construction machines have gone. Unless special care is taken to safeguard them at the very outset, heritage trees on building sites can be lost completely or, at best, seriously damaged. It is essential, therefore, that any important trees are identified at an early stage and afforded due recognition and protection during the planning process. Planting a new sapling afterwards is no cure for having thoughtlessly removed a centuries-old specimen.

Vandalism – Especially where there is uncontrolled public access, trees can suffer from wanton vandalism; for example, fire raising, bark damage and the removal of limbs. All trees are vulnerable, but veteran trees are especially defenceless. Such thoughtless actions can result in cosmetic disfigurement at best, and irreparable injury and reduced life expectancy at worst.

Damaging maintenance – Much well-intended but very damaging work has been endured by heritage trees. Misguided rescuers, who hoped to prolong the lives of these trees, might in practice have done the reverse. Antiquated practices such as filling trunk cavities with concrete, bracing limbs with chains and propping them up with iron poles are now known often to be very damaging. They can also detract from the trees' aesthetic appeal. Even today, over-zealous tree surgery, driven for the wrong reasons – such as fear of litigation, for example – can take its toll. Happily, most professional arboriculturists, using modern advances in tree care, now employ more-sensitive management practices which put tree health at the forefront.

People pressure – Because of the resulting soil compaction, repeated trampling by feet from countless visitors can bring root death and a general decline in tree health both above and below ground. Public access around well-visited specimens can mean that such trees are literally "loved to death". Fortunately, most public authorities now recognise the need to blend optimum public viewing in a safe environment with ensuring minimum tree damage, particularly in the long term.

Rural development – Serious damage can be caused by uncontrolled trampling and grazing of livestock, or by repeated deep ploughing in the vicinity of tree roots – just two of a range of pressures associated with intensive agricultural practices to which heritage trees in rural areas are vulnerable.

Pests and diseases – The threat of epidemics from introduced pests and pathogens is ever present. For example, the impact of Dutch elm disease is still being felt in Scotland,

The charred remains of the Strathleven House oak which was sadly burnt to the ground in 2004.
Vandalism is just one of the threats that heritage trees face.

having resulted in the loss of many of the county's finest trees. Many pathogens and diseases known to have caused significant losses in other countries are fortunately absent from Scotland. Britain has benefited from the protection of its island status in the past, but, as a major importer of timber today, it faces a Herculean task in trying to avoid the inadvertent introduction of a destructive insect or disease.

Pollution and climate change – Many heritage trees which have stood for centuries – or in some cases millennia – have demonstrably been able to tolerate relatively large year-to-year fluctuations in the weather. However, longer-term climate change and the effects of sustained pollution might be more invidious. Many experts believe that some species might not have the capability to tolerate profound, long-term climate change. There is a silver lining, however. Although dramatic changes in seasonal temperature and rainfall pattern might hasten the demise of some well-known species, they might also favour the growth of other, more exotic species.

What is the future for heritage trees?

The early 21st century has seen a notable and growing interest in these senior citizens of the tree world. Although some enthusiasts with an interest in heritage trees had been quietly compiling and recording information about heritage trees on an ad hoc basis for many years, it was not until relatively recently that a concerted effort was made to seek out and catalogue Scotland's heritage tree resource.

As a contribution to the Treefest Scotland 2002 campaign to celebrate Scotland's trees, woods and forests, Forestry Commission Scotland commissioned a database and Internet promotion of Scotland's heritage trees. For the first time in many years this brought together a range of information about Scotland's most remarkable and exceptional specimens, providing a unique snapshot in time. See www.forestry.gov.uk/heritagetreesscotland . The public response to this project was very encouraging. Many individuals contacted the Commission with details of trees which they believed to be special. This awareness-raising campaign unearthed some exceptional specimens previously unrecorded, including a number of hitherto unknown champion trees. The Treefest project culminated in the first "Heritage Trees of Scotland" book, published in 2003, which presented portraits of 100 of the country's most exceptional and important trees. However, that record of Scotland's heritage tree resource is by no means comprehensive or complete. Since its publication, other candidate trees have been notified to the Commission. Many of those new "finds" are profiled in these pages, whilst, sadly, other entries have been removed (see In Memoriam, page 22). Based on past experience, the authors believe that there are many more finds "out there" still waiting to be discovered, recognised and recorded.

It is only through the caring efforts of individuals, past and present, that we can enjoy these special trees today. Although some may remain in benevolent ownership, it is not enough to presume that this will always be so. It takes only one person or incident in the life of a tree to destroy it. The Tree Council, which brings together a range of organisations concerned with tree planting, care and conservation on a national basis, is advocating a system which will safeguard heritage trees for future generations, as well as providing support and advice about their care. As the United Kingdom's leading tree campaigning partnership, the Tree Council promotes the concept of protected status for "Green Monuments". This principle is not as extraordinary as it might seem. The value of important trees is already recognised in other countries, such as the Czech Republic and Poland, where all heritage trees are listed on databases and accorded special legal protection and status. In addition, they are managed in a sympathetic and sensitive manner for the benefit of future generations: a small plaque located at the side of each tree identifies it as a tree of importance. We could do the same here in Scotland, thereby recognising the undisputed historical, cultural and ecological value of these most amazing living entities.

The Dhu Loch Avenue, Inverary.

G. W. Wilson   Aberdeen

The Dhu Loch Beech Avenue near Inverary, photographed in 1870. Wilson was clearly aware of the public interest in remarkable trees during the 19th century. The avenue still exists, although many of the original trees have been lost. New trees have been planted in the gaps and a stunning group of heritage trees live on.

In Memoriam – 19th Century

    Scotland has always had a rich heritage of famous trees. In 1830 the notable artist and naturalist Jacob George Strutt (1790 - 1864) included a special section in his book 'Sylva Britannica' called Sylva Scotica, which he dedicates as a "tribute of his respect to 'A country famed for industry and song,' but also more particularly to those public-spirited noblemen and gentlemen, … who are daily consulting the interests of posterity by clothing their native hills with rich plantations, and carrying into execution every benevolent and patriotic scheme that can increase the sum of human happiness, and raise man in the scale of intellectual being." [1]

    Strutt recorded in his book 10 Scottish trees that were already famous by 1830. Eight of these have subsequently been lost over the last 175 years, but amazingly two, the Fortingall Yew (see page 148) and one of the 'Parent Larches' at Dunkeld (see page 134), have survived.

    Of the trees that have not survived, two were associated with William Wallace (see the Wallace Yew page 70), these being The Wallace Oak at Elderslie, in which tradition recalls that Wallace and 300 of his men hid amongst the branches from the English army, and The Torwood Oak, beneath which he was reputed to have made camp. The Torwood Oak was already dead before Strutt had a chance to record it, its 'last fragments carried off by pilgrims who its fame attracted'. [1]

Three wood engravings by Jacob George Strutt, clockwise from the right: The Wallace Oak, The Bishopton Sycamore and the Ash at Carnock.

The Wallace Oak

Strutt also mentions two Sycamores – The Bishopton Sycamore in Renfrewshire where Wallace was "delivered up to his enemies by the treachery of a pretended friend" [1] and the Big Tree at Kippenross, Perthshire – a sycamore so large that it measured 42 feet around, at ground level. Unfortunately this tree died in 1860 after being struck by lightning.

The other trees include a mixture of Scots pine, silver fir, wych elm and a mighty ash tree at Carnock. This was the last entry in Strutt's volume and he concludes his work on famous trees thus "Nor is it without regret that the Author sees himself arrived at the end of a task so congenial to his feelings, as that of commemorating some of those silent but happy 'inheritors of the earth', to which the shorter-lived habitants of it owe so much both of profit and enjoyment".

In Memoriam – 20th Century

As can be seen from the previous two pages, one of the issues of recording heritage trees is, because they are living organisms, they inevitably have a finite life span. Of Strutt's original 10 trees, only two survive. This does not mean that the stories of the other eight trees were not worthy of recording, but it does of course mean that their physical presence is no longer with us.

During the production of the first edition of this book and this later, much expanded edition, the authors and photographers have recorded trees that were alive when the project started in 2000 but are now deceased. One of these trees – the Wishing Tree of Argyll – was a lone, wind-blasted hawthorn growing in the wilds of Argyll. It was one of the few known 'wishing trees' in Scotland and was encrusted with coins that had been pressed into the thin bark by generations of superstitious travelers over the centuries, each coin representing a wish. It had undoubtedly been revered as a special tree for many years, as its substantial hoard of cash testified. When the original

Clockwise from the right: The Strathleven House Oak in 2003, before it was burnt down; the stump of the Newbattle Abbey Sycamore which blew down in May 2006; The Wishing Tree blown down in 2003, but then still alive.

edition of this book was published in 2003, it had unfortunately succumbed to its harsh environment and was lying prone within its enclosure. Since then the tree has died, although its remains can still be seen.

Another tree which has been lost during the 6 years of the project – The Strathleven House Oak – died in May 2004. This amazing tree, a veteran of great character, boasted the largest girth recorded for a pendunculate oak (*Quercus robur*) in Scotland, at 8.89 metres (29 feet). Unfortunately vandals set a fire in the hollow base and by the time the fire brigade arrived it was too late to save a tree that had stood on the same spot for hundreds of years.

The most recent casualty has been the Newbattle Abbey Sycamore (see page 86). This tree died on 11 May 2006, at 5pm in the afternoon, when a freak gust of wind tore through the area, resulting in this magnificent tree being blown over. Fears for the tree's long term future were expressed by the Principal of the College who, with the support of the Forestry Commission, was exploring the possibility of undertaking some tree surgery. Unfortunately, nature stepped in before any of these plans could be fulfilled.

These three examples show that our Heritage Trees are extremely vulnerable to the forces of nature, old age and human interference. It also highlights why the Tree Council's "Green Monuments" campaign is important to their future (see page 19).

Heritage Tree Legacy

Although some of our heritage trees have been lost for various reasons over the years, there are a number of ways in which their legacy can live on. Some have been written about and recorded in paintings, photographs and books (see the last 4 pages), while others have survived by being made into artefacts or relics. For example, the college who own the recently deceased Newbattle Abbey Sycamore (see page 86) intend to produce a range of items from the salvageable timber of the fallen tree, and there are hopes that something can be made from the carcass of the Strathleven House Oak (see page 22). A variety of items were made from the timber of the celebrated Corstorphine sycamore (see page 94) after it fell in a storm in 1998 – most notably a fine violin.

A tree in the Scottish Borders called the 'Union of Crowns Horse Chestnut', which was planted to mark the crowning of King James VI of Scotland as James I of England in 1603, was standing until the latter half of the twentieth century. The exact date of

the tree's death is not recorded but, once felled, somebody thought it important that this tree was not just left to rot, so they carved one of the main branches into the shape of a crocodile (see opposite). Why they did this and indeed who did it, is not known to the authors, but again the legacy of the tree lives on beyond its death.

Another way in which the memory of certain trees has survived is through vegetative regeneration. One famous case of this is the Newbattle Beech, near Dalkeith in Midlothian. Recorded in 1907 as "the most remarkable, if not the largest, of all the beeches of the spreading type now standing in Britain" [1], renowned botanist Henry Elwes (1846 – 1922) went on to photograph the tree and described the branches thus – "numerous branches which have drooped to the ground, taken root and formed a circle of subsidiary stems around the main trunk are its most peculiar feature, and may remain as large trees for centuries after the central stem decays" [1]. Elwes was a very perceptive man for a hundred years on, the main stem has decayed and been lost completely, but the tree lives on in the form of a semi-circle of layered branches, which are now magnificent trees in their own right.

Opposite: The Newbattle Beech, photographed
by Elwes in 1907, shows the "mother" tree with
the layering branches clearly apparent.
Left: The Union of Crowns Horse Chestnut.
Below: The layered branches now form a
semi-circle of 100 year old trees.

Finally, humans can play a part in conserving the genetic material that makes
heritage trees special by growing on cuttings from these famous trees and planting them
out. This has happened widely with the Corstorphine Sycamore (see page 94) and to
mark the Millennium, yew trees were planted around the country taken from cuttings
of the Fortingall Yew. These young trees carry on the tradition of their famous parents
and, perhaps as part of the future of all our heritage trees, young cuttings or saplings
should be encouraged to grow as close to their parents as is practical.

SOUTHERN SCOTLAND

Scotland's southern border brings to mind the conflict-torn "debatable lands", border ballads and tales of rieving between warring Scots and English families. Once a distant outpost of the Roman empire, today these border lands would be unrecognisable to a legionnaire. Nestled amongst the rolling uplands are large tracts of conifer forests, well-suited to the damp climate and soil, and powerhouses of sustainable timber production. But although they are highly productive, these forests' growth is inhibited by the windiness of the climate and the shallowness of the soils and, as a result, they are less suited for producing long-lived heritage trees. For these the tree lover must go northwards to the more-fertile, secluded valleys, settled by the abbeys and tamed by generations of peace-loving monks. Sir Walter Scott, who was himself a keen tree planter, loved this area and, along with other like-minded estate owners, planted and tended many trees of importance. Thus, tucked into sheltered corners of the prosperous lowlands of southern Scotland are such gems as Dawyk, Traquair and Dryburgh Abbey, each home to several noteworthy heritage trees.

Less well known is the south western corner of Scotland. Like the Borders to the east, it has plenty of character and a similarly bloody history, but a slightly more benign climate, influenced and softened by the Gulf Stream. With its undulating hills and plentiful rainfall, this region also supports ideal tree-growing conditions. Some of Scotland's largest recent plantings of spruce are to be found in Dumfries & Galloway, for example, and the Fleet woodlands are a reminder of the once widespread mixed deciduous woods which clothed these valleys of south west Scotland. The mild climate here has also helped those whose early vision created gardens of note today: tender tree species do well at places such as the Logan Botanic Gardens. The long-established and well-managed estates of Drumlanrig and Blairquhan are also places of pilgrimage for lovers of heritage trees.

Scott's View over the Tweed Valley

Southern Scotland's roads draw the traveller north towards the nation's great lowland cities: Edinburgh – the administrative capital, and Glasgow – the commercial capital. Here the landscape character suddenly changes from rural seclusion to urban bustle. In this central belt live most of Scotland's five million people, but despite human pressures, this area is home to many special heritage trees, including those of Pollok Park and Cadzow in the west, and Dalkeith Park and the Royal Botanic Garden Edinburgh in the east.

SOUTHERN SCOTLAND

Eyemouth

Dalkeith
Penicuik
Lauder
Duns

Stewarton

Irvine
Ardrossan
Troon
Prestwick
Ayr
Cumnock
Maybole
Sanquhar

Peebles
Melrose
Kelso
Galashiels
Jedburgh

Dumfries
Langholm

Stranraer

The Lochwood Oaks

A small stand of ancient sessile oaks (*Quercus petraea*) lies close to Lochwood Tower, near Moffat, Dumfries & Galloway. These trees are the surviving remnants of a long-established oak forest dating back many centuries, and include individuals of great age and character. This valuable population of veteran trees now supports an important range of wildlife and lichens.

During the 1970s, the trees at Lochwood played an important role in the development of dendrochronology: the study of annual rings to date wooden artefacts and past events. As a tree grows, it puts on a growth ring of new wood around its trunk each year. Because trees grow at different rates according to the weather, they have wider rings in favourable years and narrower rings in unfavourable years. Sequences of tree-rings thus give unique patterns which reflect changes in climate over a long period. The ring sequence, taken as a core sample, also provides a unique "fingerprint" which can be detected in other trees growing in the same geographical area.

The old oaks at Lochwood allowed scientists to construct a ring sequence from 1571 to 1970. Once this tree-ring sequence had been established, timbers in local buildings could be compared to the sequence, providing accurate dates for when the building was constructed. This technique has proved so useful that many universities and laboratories around the world are establishing their own tree ring sequences to help in the dating of wood.

Lochwood Castle, near Moffat, Dumfries & Galloway. The site is a Site of Special Scientific Interest and public access is limited.

The Drumlanrig Sycamore
and The Drumlanrig Douglas Fir

The Duke of Buccleuch's Drumlanrig Estate, near Thornhill, Dumfriesshire, is home to two of Scotland's heritage trees. One of David Douglas's (see page 112) original introductions of Douglas fir (*Pseudotsuga menziesii*) to the United Kingdom survives here. It was grown from the first seed brought into Scotland in 1827. Douglas's brother, John, was clerk of works at Drumlanrig, hence the connection. The tree is a fine specimen, with a single, straight trunk measuring 5.18 metres (17 feet) in girth and reaching 42 metres (138 feet) in height.

The second heritage tree at Drumlanrig, an imposing sycamore (*Acer pseudoplatanus*), is at least 300 years old. It has reached an immense size and has a perfect, dome-like canopy. The trunk measures 7.06 metres (23 feet) in girth and the lofty crown has attained 31.5 metres (103 feet) in height. This single tree contains 25 cubic metres (883 cubic feet) of timber, and the canopy covers 800 square metres (8611 square feet).

Sycamore, also known in Scotland as plane or plain, was a popular species by the mid–17th century. The 6th Earl of Haddington wrote in 1761 that "there is no old seat, no gentleman's house, nor any place where old trees are, but the plains are the most numerous". [1]

The Douglas fir stands in a small woodland to the north of Drumlanrig Castle, while the sycamore is in parkland close to the castle and its main access drive. The castle is off the A76 road about 4.8 kilometres (3 miles) north of Thornhill, Dumfries & Galloway. The grounds are open to the public and admission charges apply.

Blairquhan Dool Tree

The "dool" or "dule" trees were trees used as natural gallows for hanging criminals. They were common features on many estates until the middle of the 18th century. Such trees normally occupied a prominent location near the laird's residence, where the corpse was left to swing as a deterrent for all to see. The favoured species used for this purpose was sycamore, because its strong and resilient timber was unlikely to fail at the crucial moment. The word "dool" derives from old Scots and means sorrowful or mournful.

One of Scotland's few surviving dool trees is the ancient sycamore (*Acer pseudoplatanus*) that stands in the shadow of Blairquhan Castle, near Straiton, Ayrshire. The tree is thought to have been planted early in the 16th century during the reign of King James V of Scotland. The moss-covered trunk has a girth of 5.6 metres (18 feet 4 inches), and is completely hollow, with only a very thin outer shell of sound wood supporting the tree. The once spreading crown was heavily pruned in 1997 in an effort to preserve the fragile shell and prevent the much-weakened trunk from total collapse. Vigorous new growth is now establishing a new, smaller crown. This unwitting instrument of execution will remain in the land of the living for a while yet.

Close to Blairquhan House, Blairquhan Estate, off the B741 road about 1.6 kilometres (1 mile) west of Straiton, South Ayrshire. The house and grounds are open to the public during the last two weeks of July and the first two weeks of August, or by appointment. Admission charges apply.

Rabbie Burns' Sycamore

Robert Burns
(1759 - 1796)

The fine, large sycamore (*Acer pseudoplatanus*) that dominates Alloway Auld Kirk, built in 1516, has taken the name of Scotland's National Bard. Robert Burns, who was born a stone's throw from the kirk, was inspired by this eerie setting, and later immortalised the kirk in his famous work,
Tam O' Shanter:

> *"When, glimmering through the groaning trees,*
> *Kirk-Alloway seem'd in a bleeze,*
> *Through ilka bore the beams were glancing,*
> *And loud resounding mirth and dancing."*

The grand and imposing sycamore, which appears to emerge from the foundations of the ancient church, certainly adds to the atmosphere. The shapely, spreading crown is 22.5 metres (74 feet) tall and the single, squat trunk has a girth of 3.8 metres (12 feet 6 inches). At some time in the past the church wall has been carefully bridged over the swollen root buttresses to accommodate its ever-increasing girth. Its date of origin and its provenance are unknown, although judging by its dimensions, it probably began growing in the 18th century.

It is tempting to imagine that this gentle giant that now watches over "Alloway's Auld Haunted Kirk" was around when the young Burns began writing poems inspired by the natural world around him.

Next to the ruins of Alloway Auld Kirk, in the village of Alloway on the southern outskirts of Ayr, South Ayrshire. Free public access is available throughout the year.

The Auld Yew Tree of Loudoun

This ancient yew (*Taxus baccata*) stands in the shadow of the ruined walls of Loudon Castle, near Galston, East Ayrshire. It is said that one of the Loudoun family charters was signed under the yew in the time of William the Lionheart (1165 - 1214), and that the drafts of the Treaty of Union with England in 1603 were negotiated and discussed under its canopy. [1]

When Lord James of Loudon went into voluntary exile in Holland, he devised a cunning method of corresponding with his family back on his estate. For fear of detection, he addressed his letters to "The Gudewife of Auldton, at the Auld Yew Tree of Loudoun". Remarkably, they always reached their intended destination. [1]

The trunk of the yew measures 5.34 metres (17 feet 6 inches) in girth. When the original castle, dating from the 15th century, was heavily extended in 1811, the walls came within two metres of the trunk, and have left the crown very one-sided.

The tree is clearly a great survivor. In December 1941 the castle was gutted by a fire which started in the bedroom of Countess Edith Loudoun. Fourteen fire engines from surrounding towns reached the blaze, but it was already too late, and the castle has remained a ruin ever since. How the yew survived the inferno is a mystery.

On the south façade of the impressive ruin of Loudon Castle, off the A719 road about 1.6 kilometres (1 mile) north of Galston, East Ayrshire. The castle now forms the centrepiece of a theme park which is open to the public from April to October.

The Dawyck Silver Fir
and the Dawyck Beech

Unsurprisingly, some of Scotland's heritage trees grace some of the country's fine botanic gardens, and the Dawyck Botanic Garden, near Peebles, is particularly generously endowed. The European silver fir (*Abies alba*) with the earliest known planting date in Scotland stands here. This was reputed to have been planted in 1680 by the Veitch family. Despite the crown now looking rather tattered and straggly, this is still a fine example of Europe's principal fir. Its trunk measures 5.4 metres (17 feet 9 inches) in girth and its height is recorded as 35 metres (115 feet).

The silver fir was introduced to the United Kingdom from central Europe in 1603 (see page 195). It grows well in Scotland and was widely planted during the 18th and 19th centuries.

Meanwhile, just next door in the private garden of Dawyck House, is the Dawyck Beech (*Fagus sylvatica* 'Dawyck'), which takes its name from the Peeblesshire estate where it was first discovered. While planting a beech wood in 1860, a sharp-eyed forester noticed a single sapling with an unusual form, its branches sweeping tightly upwards. The laird, Sir John Murray Naesmyth (1803 - 1876) had it replanted in the policy woodlands near Dawyck House. When the estate changed hands in 1897, it was the new owner, F R S Balfour, who brought this natural mutant to popular attention, so that by 1912 it was officially referred to as Dawyck Beech. The original tree still stands in good health and has retained its upright form and spire-like crown.

The silver fir stands in Dawyck Botanic Garden, off the B712 road about 11.3 kilometres (7 miles) south west of Peebles, Scottish Borders, while the beech can readily be viewed from the botanic garden. The garden is a specialist outpost of the Royal Botanic Garden Edinburgh.

The Kailzie Larch

The 1725 Larches

wo survivors of the original European larches (*Larix decidua*) introduced to Scotland in 1725 by Sir James Naesmyth stand in separate gardens near Peebles in the Scottish Borders. These are two of the earliest surviving plantings in Scotland of a species that was ultimately to have a major impact on commercial forestry in the United Kingdom.

One, the Dawyck Larch, stands in Dawyck Botanic Garden. Now measuring 4.46 metres (14 feet 7 inches) in girth and 33 metres (108 feet) tall, it is still a fine tree.

The Dawyck Larch

Sir James Naesmyth (1644 – 1754), Laird of Posso and Dawyck, was a renowned collector of trees from around the world, and his early plantings were to establish the fine collection that forms Dawyck Botanic Garden today.

The other, the Kailzie Larch, is one of the finest specimens, and can be found at Kailzie Gardens, near Peebles. The larch's introduction to the estate was amusingly recounted by a member of the Innerleithen Alpine Club following a visit to the estate in 1890:

"In 1725, on returning from London, Sir James brought with him in his carriage some young larches, and he called in passing and dined with his friend the Laird of Kailzie. This Laird of Posso and Dawyck, like his father 'The Deil', had trees on the brain and no doubt over the wine waxed eloquent about the new importation. The result was that one specimen was planted next morning in Kailzie Park, and is still standing there, growing vigorously and without symptom of decay. Its height is 105 feet and its circumference four feet from the ground is twelve feet." [1]

The straight, unblemished trunk now measures 4.8 metres (15 feet 9 inches) in girth at 1.2 metres (4 feet) above the ground, a respectable increase of 1.1 metres (3 feet 9 inches) since 1890. It supports a crown which has developed huge, up-curved limbs typically seen in many old larches.

Dawyck Botanic Garden is off the B712 road about 11.3 kilometres (7 miles) south west of Peebles, Scottish Borders. Public access is available from mid-February until mid-November. The garden is a specialist offshoot of the Royal Botanic Garden Edinburgh.

Kailzie Gardens is off the B7062 road about 4.8 kilometres (3 miles) south east of Peebles. The garden is open to the public seven days a week throughout the year.

The Capon Tree

The Capon Tree, a hollow pedunculate or "English" oak (*Quercus robur*), is one of the last survivors of the ancient Jed Forest. About 800 years old, this celebrated tree has been a constant feature in the turbulent history of the border country. The origin of the tree's name is uncertain, but it could have been derived from the word "capuche", the hood worn by the monks who sheltered under its branches on their way to the nearby Jedburgh Abbey.

According to tradition, border clans rallied for action at the tree during the troubled days of the 16th century. Living in a border town, Jedburgh's local families were involved in fighting the English, and the Jethart Callants had a reputation for outstanding bravery. Both they and the Capon Tree are celebrated annually at the Jedburgh Callants' Festival. Each July the "Callant", a young man chosen to represent the town, leads his mounted cavalcade on historic rides, the most important being to Redeswire to commemorate the last cross-border skirmish. On Festival Day, the Callant visits Ferniehurst Castle, and on his return home stops at the Capon Tree, taking a sprig and wearing it in the lapel of his jacket.

A wood engraving of the tree, taken from Selby's "British Forest Trees", 1842.

On the banks of the River Jed and alongside the A68 less than 3 kilometres (2 miles) south of Jedburgh town centre, accessible by a 15-minute walk from the town on pavements all the way, starting from the first bridge (near the Abbey). The tree is around the corner on the right just after the third bridge.

The Posso Sycamores

The Posso Sycamores (*Acer pseudoplatanus*) are a pair of magnificent trees standing in a remote Peeblesshire glen close to the ruins of 16th century Posso Tower.

One specimen close to the tower boasts the title of the largest-girthed sycamore recorded in the United Kingdom, its trunk measuring an astonishing 8.54 metres (28 feet) in girth. Large buttress roots sprawl over the uneven ground and between the scattered masonry of the tower.

Its partner stands isolated in the middle of a grazed field, with a perfectly symmetrical crown. Although its girth is smaller, its girth is still an impressive 7.06 metres (23 feet), and the crown reaches a height of 27.5 metres (90 feet).

Privately owned farmland about 200 metres (220 yards) west of Posso Farm farmhouse. The farm is about 8 kilometres (5 miles) along an unclassifed road that runs south towards Kirkton Manor and Posso from a junction with the A72 about 2.4 kilometres (1.5 miles) west of Peebles. Access is available only with permission.

King of The Wood

Hidden up a small wooded glen in rural border country stands a fine oak (*Quercus robur*) which rejoices in the regal title of King of the Woods. A handsome and imposing individual, it boasts a single, straight trunk furnished by a deep, well-formed crown which ascends to a height of 24 metres (79 feet). The stout bole, clean and branch-free for a length of 13 metres (43 feet), has a girth of 5.42 metres (17 feet 9 inches), and is punctuated by a massive burr at its base.

This named tree was already a notable specimen by the middle of the 19th century, when Selby, in his 1842 book "British Forest Trees", described it as:

"…a beautiful oak of vigorous growth, with a trunk 43 feet in height and a circumference of upwards of 16 feet…" [1]

Another reference to the Tree in the Penny Magazine 1842 describes the tree thus:

"In Roxburghshire, near Jedburgh, on the estate of the Marquess of Lothian, stands a remarkable oak, called the King of the Woods. It is now [January 19, 1837] sixteen feet six inches in circumference, at one foot from the ground; its whole height is seventy-three feet; the height of the trunk, before it forms branches, is forty-three feet; and it is as straight as, and something of the form of, a wax candle. It is, perhaps, the finest piece of oak timber in Scotland; and its beauty has probably saved it from the axe." [2]

The origin and age of the oak is unknown, although it is clearly of some antiquity. It stands proudly at the top of a steeply sided glen formed by a small burn, amidst mature, mixed woodland, itself a small, semi-natural remnant of the once-extensive oakwoods which clothed the fertile land of the Borders in past millennia. Spared the woodsman's axe, it has been allowed to achieve its impressive dimensions and deserved regal status. It continues to flourish to this day, an outstanding example of its species.

The tree is in woodland less than 3 kilometres (2 miles) south of Jedburgh. Accessible via an unsigned public footpath off the A68, immediately opposite the Capon Tree (see page 44). The path passes by the base of the tree approximately 200 metres (220 yards) from the main road, and is clearly labelled. The tree is owned by Lothian Estates.

The King James II Holly

The expansive parkland of Floors Castle, on the banks of the River Tweed, boasts many fine trees. One of these is a solitary and conspicuous holly (*Ilex aquifolium*) which commemorates a tragic moment in Scotland's history: it is said to mark the very spot where King James II of Scotland (1430 - 1460) died in an unfortunate accident.

King James II was an enthusiast of modern artillery and had a large collection of cannon, which he used to good effect in his many campaigns. In 1460, while laying siege to nearby Roxburgh Castle, one of the last Scottish castles held by the English after the Wars of Independence, a cannon loaded with too much powder exploded. A large shard of wood severed the King's leg and he bled to death very quickly. The Fife chronicler Robert Lindsay of Pitscottie (c. 1532 - 1580) graphically records the incident in his "Historie and Chronicles of Scotland, 1436 - 1565":

"…his thigh-bone was dung in two with a piece of misframed gun that brake in shooting, by the which he was stricken to the ground and died hastily."

The solitary holly is a living reminder of this untimely end to the monarch's reign. The tree is enclosed by a stock fence, and displays a typically bushy, if windswept crown. Several well-established suckers appear to emerge from a decayed stump, suggesting that this modest heritage tree is older than it first appears.

Floors Castle, the largest inhabited castle in Scotland, has been the ancestral home of the Dukes of Roxburghe since it was built in 1721.

Floors Castle and estate lie on the western edge of Kelso, Scottish Borders. It is well-signposted from the town and its approach roads. The castle and grounds are open to the public daily from April to October. Admission charges apply. The holly tree stands on the open parkland to the south west of the castle, on the riverside walk by the banks of the River Tweed.

Hirsel Sycamore

The handsome sycamore (*Acer pseudoplatanus*) which stands proudly at the Hirsel, on the outskirts of Coldstream, is said to have been planted to commemorate the poor souls who perished in the Battle of Flodden in 1513. Flodden Field, the site of the conflict, lies only 6.4 kilometres (4 miles) away over the English border. There, a huge Scottish army, intent on invading England, suffered an ignominious defeat at the hands of the English in a bloody battle which was to become a turning point in Scotland's turbulent history. King James IV of Scotland led the Scottish invasion force, only to be killed in the fray, leaving only an 18 month old baby as his heir and a crisis for the kingdom.

The sycamore is an exceptionally large specimen with a short, stout trunk of 6.5 metres (21 feet 4 inches) in girth. This supports a capacious, billowing dome 28 metres (92 feet) in height, formed by many huge, upswept limbs, themselves the size of mature trees. The remarkable architecture of this mighty tree is the epitomy of strength, and the tree is in good heart.

Regrettably, it has suffered from some unwelcome and unnecessary attention in the past. The remains of old chains, presumably installed with the intention of holding the tree together, now garrotte the main limbs and create zones of weakness. This crude attempt was superseded by a more modern, but already outdated system of cable bracing, which criss-crosses between the limb structure. This unsightly tangle of metalwork is unnecessary and ineffectual in this case, and only serves to inflict undesirable injury and detract from the natural beauty of the tree.

> The tree is in Hirsel Country Park, on the northern outskirts of Coldstream, Scottish Borders. Signposted access is off the A697. The sycamore stands just outside the walled garden, at its south east corner. The country park is open for public access throughout the year. Parking charges apply.

Hirsel Tulip Tree

According to John Evelyn in 1664, the first tulip trees (*Liriodendron tulipifera*) were brought to Britain "by John Tradescant, under the name of the Tulip-tree (from the likeness of its flowers)" about the middle of the 17th century. Evelyn continues that the leaves of the tree are "of a very peculiar shape, as if the points were cut off", [1] which is an accurate description of this particular species.

Unfortunately the exact date of introduction is somewhat uncertain, although it was grown by Bishop Compton at Fulham in 1688. One of the earliest trees was in the gardens of the Earl of Peterborough at Parsons Green, Fulham, and was described in 1776 as "an old tree quite destroyed by others which overhang it." [2] Unfortunately, most of the early trees have gone, but one that remains is the impressive specimen still growing in the grounds of the Hirsel in Coldstream.

In 1840 Loudon referred to the "Hirsel Tulip Tree at the seat of the Earl of Home", which was at that time "100 years old and 20 feet in girth 3 feet from the ground". [3] This puts the planting date of the tree around 1740, making it perhaps one of the oldest specimens still standing.

Elwes and Henry in 1907 were in communication with Mr. Cairns, head gardener at the Hirsel, and by 1903, "it was slowly decaying, some of the larger branches being gone, but that what remained carry a large amount of healthy foliage, and flowers more or less every year". [4]

This remarkable tree was still in good health in the spring of 2006, although the walled garden around the tree has now been abandoned. This has the peculiar effect of leaving this fine specimen growing in what feels like a wasteland. The tree with its hollow stem now has a girth of nearly 7.8 metres (26 feet) at 1.2 metres (4 feet) above the ground, and is a fantastic example of its type.

The tree is in Hirsel Country Park, on the northern outskirts of Coldstream, Scottish Borders. Sign-posted access is off the A697. The tulip tree stands in the middle of the walled garden. The country park is open for public access throughout the year. Parking charges apply.

The Dryburgh Abbey Yew

RUINS OF DRYBURGH ABBEY.

Within the tranquil ruins of Dryburgh Abbey, near the Border town of St Boswells, stands an ancient yew (*Taxus baccata*). It is alleged to have been planted by monks in 1136, thus predating the foundation of the Abbey by Hugh de Moreville in 1150. Nestling in a fertile loop of the River Tweed, the site has a long history as a place of Christian worship, extending back to the dark ages when it was associated with the little known Saint Modan, a follower of Saint Columba. The planting of yew trees at places of religious worship was common practice at the time. Despite the abbey's turbulent history of fire and destruction, the solitary yew has survived unscathed.

The yew is an unassuming specimen of no significant size, with a trunk girth of 3.86 metres (12 feet 8 inches). Historical girth measurements indicate a very slow rate of growth. Sir David Erskine, a previous owner of the Dryburgh Yew, recorded its girth at 10 feet (measured at 6 feet above ground) in 1826; while in 1894, John Lowe found it to be 11 feet 4 inches.[1] Despite its relatively modest dimensions, it would seem feasible that the yew could indeed have originated in the 12th century.

The private grounds of Dryburgh Abbey House, St Boswells, Scottish Borders. It can easily be viewed from the adjacent grounds of the Abbey itself, which is in the care of Historic Scotland, and to which public access is available all year.

The Covin Tree

A "covin" tree traditionally stood at the front of a Scottish castle or stately home, and was where the laird met and received his guests. One of the few surviving covin trees stands on the lawns in front of Bemersyde House, ancestral seat of the Haig family. It is a fine, old sweet chestnut (*Castanea sativa*) brimming with character, and still acts as a natural focal point to this day.

The lands of Bemersyde have been held by the Haig family since 1162. It is said that the tree was planted at that time by Petrus de Haga, the founder of the family, and it has flourished ever since. The tree is certainly of great age and must have been an impressive specimen in its prime. Time, however, has taken its toll and the centre of the original tree has died. Fortunately, before the tree's demise, the present Earl had the foresight to propagate it by layering some of the lower branches. The vast, decaying hulk of the old tree now stands surrounded by vigorous offshoots. Old iron rings on the branches of the original tree are a reminder that this was once a formidable specimen: these were formerly attached to concrete weights in an attempt to balance the huge trunk.

The Covin Tree has been a feature of Bemersyde for many years, and appears in many paintings of the house, including one by J M W Turner (1775 - 1851) which is now in the safekeeping of the British Museum in London.

Bemersyde House is approximately 4.8 kilometres (3 miles) east of Melrose, Scottish Borders, on the east bank of the River Tweed. It is accessible off minor roads approximately 1.6 kilometres (1 mile) north of Dryburgh Abbey. Bemersyde Gardens are open from mid-April to mid-October, from 10am to 4pm. Opening times are indicated by a sign outside the gates to the house and admission charges apply.

Adam and Eve

A pair of the earliest Sitka spruce (*Picea sitchensis*) introduced to Great Britain are, appropriately, called "Adam and Eve". These were supposedly acquired by Culzean estate in 1836, only four years after the species was introduced to these shores from its native North America by the intrepid botanist and explorer, David Douglas (see also the Fairburn Sitka, page 222 and the Drumtochty Sitka, page 210). Grown in pots for the first 15 years, they were planted out within the area known as Happy Valley, part of the extensive landscaped grounds of Culzean Castle, in 1851. The trees stand 70 metres (77 yards) apart, and now form the focal point of an interesting collection of conifers, many from the New World, which was established in the latter part of the 19th century.

The trees form a fine pair and have been allowed to develop well-shaped, conical crowns typical of the species. Despite being badly attacked by spruce aphid several years ago, which caused extensive defoliation, the trees have recovered well and display full, healthy crowns. The single, straight trunks are typically swollen and enlarged at the base, a common feature of many old Sitka.

It is Eve, the northernmost of the pair, which is the larger, measuring 5.41 metres (17 feet 9 inches) in girth and 45m (147 feet 8 inches) in height. Adam's statistics are slightly less impressive, at 5.13 metres (16 feet 10 inches) in girth, and a height of 39 metres (128 feet).

The trees stand in Culzean Castle Country Park, on the Ayrshire coast approximately 19 kilometres (12 miles) south of Ayr. It is well sign-posted off the A719. The trees stand in the area known as Happy Valley, and are sign-posted. A property of the National Trust for Scotland, the Country Park is open daily throughout the year. Admission charges apply.

The Colliers' Oak

The Colliers' Oak (*Quercus robur*) is a well-known landmark in the Ayrshire town of Dailly, a living reminder of the area's long and illustrious association with the mining industry. Standing a stone's throw from the ruins of Dalquharran Castle, it might mark the spot where coal was first discovered in the area. It acquired its name because, according to tradition, the Laird of Dalquharran and the colliers used to convene under the shade of the old oak to discuss business and settle matters of common interest. [1] The area was a thriving mining community for many years and produced thousands of tons of coal. In 1896 Dalquharran pit employed 94 underground workers and a further 22 on the surface. The pit eventually closed in 1977.

The tree is a squat, compact specimen no greater than 12 metres (39 feet) in height and appears to have been pollarded in the past. The trunk, which is heavily burred, measures 5.64 metres (18 feet 6 inches) in girth. Despite a large cavity in the base of the trunk, it is in good health, and forms an attractive feature in the landscape surrounding the castle.

The local mining industry has long since ceased to exist, and miners no longer meet under the leafy boughs. However, the old oak remains a much-loved resident of the town, and features in the crest of the local primary school.

Approximately 1.6 kilometres (1 mile) north of the town of Dailly, South Ayrshire, on private roads off the B741. The tree stands next to an old track approximately 250 metres north of the ruins of Dalquharran Castle.

Palms at Logan

It is with good reason that Logan Botanic Garden is often referred to as "Scotland's most exotic garden". Nestling on the peninsula known as the Rhinns of Galloway at the most south westerly tip of the Scottish mainland, it enjoys the warming influence of the Gulf Stream and experiences exceptionally mild winters. As a result, a remarkable collection of exotic plants, many from the Southern Hemisphere, flourishes in the benign climate. Indeed, such is the impressive display that it is hard to imagine one is in Scotland.

The garden is renowned for its palm trees and tree ferns, which collectively create a striking feature and lend the garden a sub-tropical atmosphere. Towering, 130-year-old tree ferns (*Dicksonia antarctica*), from Tasmania, stand side by side with spiky-leaved cabbage palms (*Cordyline australis*) from New Zealand. Many of these survive from the time of the garden's establishment in 1869 by Agnes Buchan-Hepburn, a keen amateur gardener who liked to experiment with newly introduced tender species from exotic climes. The palms and ferns have thrived ever since, only occasionally getting frosted back in especially hard winters.

The short avenue of Chusan palms (*Trachycarpus fortunei*), the only species of true palm hardy in Scotland, provides an arresting feature by the stream. This species was introduced to the United Kingdom from China in 1849 by the renowned Scottish plant hunter, Robert Fortune (1812 - 1880). Its common name refers to Chusan Island (now Zhoushan Island), where Fortune first discovered the species which was subsequently named after him. Strictly speaking, the Chusan palm is not a tree, because its trunk is largely composed of the compacted bases of the discarded fan-shaped leaves. Once formed, it does not increase in girth.

Main picture: Chusan palms (*Trachycarpus fortunei*). Inset: tree ferns (*Dicksonia antarctica*).

Logan Botanic Garden is approximately 22.4 kilometres (14 miles) south of Stranraer, Dumfries & Galloway, on the B7065 road. The garden is a specialist garden of the Royal Botanic Garden Edinburgh, and has been in its care since 1969. The gardens are open daily from 1 March to 31 October and admission charges apply.

Traquair House Yews

Four ancient yew trees (*Taxus baccata*) stand in the grounds of historic Traquair House, near the Borders town of Innerleithen. Dating from the early 12th century, Traquair House is reputed to be the oldest continuously inhabited dwelling in Scotland. It has been visited by many of Scotland's prominent historical figures, including Mary, Queen of Scots and Bonnie Prince Charlie.

Forming a close group near the banks of the Quair Water (which had flooded just before the photographs were taken), the four yews are of outlandish shape and form. Their hunched and twisted limbs give the impression of four old men bent over in discussion, and the dark inner cavern formed by their dense foliage is eerily atmospheric.

On the edge of woodland and next to a footpath along the banks of the Quair Water east of Traquair House, about 1.6 kilometres (1 mile) south of Innerleithen, Scottish Borders. Traquair House is open to the public from mid-April to the end of October.

The Tinnis Ash

In a pasture about 30 metres (33 yards) south of the A708 road, 8 kilometres (5 miles) west of Selkirk, Scottish Borders. Access is available only with permission.

What is probably Scotland's oldest ash tree (*Fraxinus excelsior*) forms part of an important remnant of wood pasture in Bowhill Estate, near Selkirk. The partially collapsed remains of this once exceptionally large specimen are still very much alive, and this ancient veteran continues to thrive in its rural setting. The trunk might have originally measured between 9 and 10 metres (30 and 33 feet) in girth before it became so rotten that it eventually collapsed and part was lost. The remaining fragments present an intriguing framework of sculptural beauty. Ash as a species is not known for its longevity or great size. However, in exceptional circumstances, it is clearly capable of both.

Yester's Lime Avenue

One of the oldest known planting of common lime (*Tilia × europaea*) in Scotland is the splendid avenue laid out in 1680 which leads to the ornate gates of Yester House in Gifford, East Lothian. This runs in a perfectly straight line for 400 metres (437 yards) and comprises a total of 59 trees: 29 down one side of the road and 27 down the other. These are laid out at a regular spacing of 10m (11 yards) between rows and 7 metres (7.65 yards) between the trees within each row.

The entire avenue is remarkably intact for its age, and has suffered only one or two recent losses, caused by storm damage. Yester's Lime Avenue forms a hugely impressive and much-loved feature in the village landscape.

The avenue lines a public road in the heart of Gifford, East Lothian. It runs from the Tweeddale Arms Hotel on the High Street to the gates of Yester Estate, and can be readily viewed from several vantage points within the village. Access to Yester Estate is strictly prohibited.

Considerable variation exists between the individual trees forming the avenue in terms of girth and height. The largest specimen is near the western gate-house and has a girth of 5.18 metres (17 feet). Typically, old limes rarely attain the large girths of other broadleaved species of similar age, and even very old trees can have deceptively small trunks.

Common lime is a natural hybrid of the small-leaved lime (*Tilia cordata*) and the large-leaved lime (*Tilia platyphyllos*). Although widely planted, it suffers from a major drawback which is the bane of those who maintain them. It has a natural propensity to produce masses of epicormic growth on the trunk and within the lower crown which, if left unchecked, develop into dense and impenetrable thickets of twiggy sprouts. Regular pruning is required every two years or so to keep the growth in check if a clean and visible trunk is desired. Fortunately, this onerous task has been regularly carried out on the Yester avenue, so that the full impact of their trunks can be appreciated.

The Polwarth Thorn

The Borders village of Polwarth was abandoned long ago and little evidence of it remains. However, the famous Polwarth hawthorn (*Crataegus monogyna*), once a centrepiece on the village green, survives. For centuries, newly married couples would dance around the tree, which was immortalised by poet Allan Ramsay (1686 – 1758) in "Polwarth, On The Green":

In Polwarth, 8 kilometres (5 miles) south west of Duns, Scottish Borders. Turn off the A6105 road at a sign for Polwarth. After 400 metres (440 yards), take a right-hand fork. The tree is in a new residential development. Public access is available.

> *"At Polwarth on the Green,*
> *If you'll meet me in the morn,*
> *Where lads and lasses do convene*
> *To dance around the thorn."*

The original tree has died, but it has been replaced by its own saplings, two of which, enclosed by iron railings, still occupy the site.

Hawthorn is associated with pagan Mayday rites, and blossoms of "the May" are said to symbolise love, betrothal and fertility.

The Prestonhall Beech

One of the largest known beech trees (*Fagus sylvatica*) in Scotland is the fine, open-grown specimen that stands in parkland close to Prestonhall House, near Pathhead, Midlothian. The tree is more than 30 metres (98 feet) tall and its immense trunk measures 6.69 metres (22 feet) in girth. This tree is a first-class example of a species that was planted on many country estates, and which grows particularly well in the fertile lands of Lothian.

Beech as a species is not renowned for its longevity, and few trees exceed 250 years old before decay takes its toll.

The Wallace Yew

The Wallace Statue, high above the Tweed Valley, near Dryburgh.

Of all the trees associated with Scotland's popular hero, William Wallace (c.1270 - 1305), it is the old yew (*Taxus baccata*) at Elderslie in Renfrewshire that is the most legitimate contender. Known locally as the Wallace Yew, it stands near the ruined house where Wallace was reputed to have been born.

Local legend has it that the tree was a sapling when Wallace was born, and that he played in its branches as child. However, although the tree is of considerable antiquity, it is unlikely to have existed in Wallace's day. A more plausible theory is that it was grown from a seed or shoot of an ancient yew that did stand in Wallace's time. With a girth of 4.3 metres (14 feet) and height of 12 metres (39 feet), the tree has been estimated to be between 350 and 400 years old.

The yew has been sorely neglected and abused in the past and a fire set by vandals in 1978 all but killed it. A restoration programme implemented by Renfrewshire Council was bringing about a slow but sure recovery, but exceptional gales on the 12th of January 2005 proved too much for the decayed trunk, and a large section was torn off and lost. The tree still stands, albeit in a diminished state. Like Wallace, this tree is a fighter and could be around for a while yet.

A small public park in Elderslie, Renfrewshire, at the junction of Main Road and Wallace Avenue. Free public access is available throughout the year.

EASTERN AND CENTRAL SCOTLAND

Like its other compass points, Scotland's eastern region is an area of striking contrasts. Coastal Angus and Aberdeenshire provide a home to fertile farms and estates, whilst to the north, great rivers such as the Dee, the Don and Spey carry rainfall away from the central Cairngorms massif. These river systems intersect many beautiful wooded landscapes: places such as Abernethy and Mar Lodge support iconic forests of Caledonian Scots pine, silver birch, alder and other native species – remnants of Scotland's great original wildwood. One example, Royal Deeside, is home to some of Scotland's oldest and largest Caledonian pine. But the east of Scotland is also more prone to frosts and harsher weather than the more-gentle west, and growing conditions here are drier too. Leith Hall and Glamis are favourite places of pilgrimage for heritage tree seekers, but many of the best examples of heritage trees in the east are more widely scattered than in southern and central Scotland.

Central Scotland in general – and Highland Perthshire in particular – is the epicentre for lovers of heritage trees. Since the days of the visionary "improving lairds" with their great estates such as Atholl, this part of Scotland has had a long and illustrious tradition of introducing new species and carefully tending them. Famous sons of Scotland, such as David Douglas and John Jeffries, brought seed from the Pacific northwest of Canada and America, and these exotic species thrived in their new habitat. If you only have time to visit one part of the country, go to Scotland's "Big Tree Country", and in particular the Tay valley. Around Dunkeld the heritage tree enthusiast will encounter a large number of extraordinary trees, such as the Dunkeld Douglas, the Birnam Sycamore and Oak, the Parent Larch and the Hermitage Douglas. Diana's Grove at Blair Atholl contains a unique collection of gigantic specimens. This part of Scotland is a place of pilgrimage where you can absorb the character and atmosphere of these amazing living giants. Just to the west, near Kenmore, is Europe's oldest living thing, the renowned Fortingall Yew, whilst to the east, Europe's tallest beech hedge, the Meikleour Beech Hedge, is close to Blairgowrie. In fact, this corner of Scotland boasts more heritage trees than anywhere else in Scotland.

Stand of aspen in Aberdeenshire

EASTERN & CENTRAL SCOTLAND

Brechin
59
Montrose

Pitlochry
77
84
81
76
78
Aberfeldy Blairgowrie
80 79 83 82 75
65
66 67
74 69 71
72
73

Forfar
62
63
60

Arbroath
61

Perth
64
48
55
54
53
70
56
Crieff
68
49
Auchtermuchty
44
57
45
Dundee
58
Tayport
50
51 52
St Andrews
46 47

Dollar
Glenrothes
Alloa
42
43
73
41
Edinburgh
37
39
36 38 29 35
40 28 34
30
31
32
Dunbar
33

The Roslin Sweet Chestnut

An ancient sweet chestnut (*Castanea sativa*) stands in woodland near the mysterious Rosslyn Chapel in the Midlothian village of Roslin. Its vast and heavily burred trunk has an impressive girth of 7.72 metres (25 feet 4 inches), one of the largest in Scotland. The crown consists of a contorted framework of large, skeletal limbs, and only the occasional sprig of live foliage and vigorous basal shoots continues to keep this time-weary veteran alive. The encroaching growth of surrounding young trees is slowly but surely starting to over-shadow and engulf this once open-grown specimen.

This chestnut is probably between 400 and 450 years old. It stands next to the moss-covered ruins of Rosebank House, once the residence of the Dowager Countess of Rosslyn. The house is also noteworthy as the birthplace of the poet, author and songwriter, Hector McNeill (1746 - 1818).

The chestnut was clearly a much cherished feature of the property in its time. Two specially crafted iron bands encircle one of the main limbs in a vain attempt to stop it collapsing.

In Roslin, Midlothian. Head for the signs to Rosslyn Chapel. Continue on the road for 130 metres (142 yards) past the chapel entrance and visitor centre, and turn right on to a track just before Slatebarns Caravan Site. At 55 metres (60 yards), take the right-hand fork and continue along the woodland path for a further 240 metres (262 yards). The tree stands 30 metres (33 yards) into young woodland on the left-hand side of the path.

Rizzio's Chestnut

Melville Castle was frequented by Mary, Queen of Scots. During one of her visits, David Rizzio, her Italian secretary and close companion, is said to have planted a tree as a token of his love for her by the banks of the River North Esk. The tree, an ancient sweet chestnut (*Castanea sativa*), survives to this day next to the stable block, now known appropriately as Chestnut House.

Mary, Queen of Scots
(1542 - 1587)

However, such blatant displays of love were to be Rizzio's downfall. He was murdered before the Queen's eyes in the Palace of Holyrood House in 1566 by a group of conspirators led by Mary's jealous second husband, Lord Darnley. Rizzio's chestnut remains today as an enduring symbol of his ill-fated affection for Mary.

The tree is a fine old specimen of huge girth, and it is quite feasible that it did indeed originate in the mid-1560s. The vast trunk is 7.6 metres (25 feet) in girth. Like all ancient sweet chestnuts, it is of no significant height, and has died back to 16.7 metres (55 feet). The crown is of reasonable shape, although abundant deadwood indicates that it is in the natural process of decline. However, the capacity for the species to regenerate itself by forming a new crown from dormant buds should guarantee its presence for a few more centuries at least.

The private garden of Chestnut House, about 100 metres (110 yards) south west of Melville Castle Hotel, near Dalkeith, Midlothian. Access to the tree itself is available only with written permission. However, it can be viewed from the grounds of the hotel.

The Great Yew of Ormiston

Early woodcut of John Knox
(c.1514 - 1572),
from Beza's *Icones* (1580)

This is a first-class example of the few "layering" yews (*Taxus baccata*) known in Scotland. Weeping branches radiate out from the solid central trunk and take root where they touch the ground, encircling the tree in an ever-extending fringe of growth. The inner chamber formed by the layered branches and dense foliage creates a spacious, natural cathedral of arching limbs. The huge central trunk measures 6.9 metres (22 feet 10 inches) in girth. Records of measurement over the past 160 years suggest a very slow rate of increment, and it is perfectly possible that the tree could be as old as 1000 years.

As early as the 15th century the yew was recognised as a local landmark: a parchment dated 1474, found among some old papers belonging to the Earl of Hopetoun, had been signed under the yew tree. [1]

The famous religious reformer, John Knox, who was born in nearby Haddington, is also reputed to have preached his early sermons within the secluded interior of the yew's evergreen canopy. Here Knox, along with his influential mentor, George Wishart, sowed the seeds of the Reformation, which was ultimately to sweep throughout Scotland.

Profuse regeneration
from the layering
boughs.

A private residential development close to the ruins of Ormiston Hall, Ormiston, East Lothian. It is reached from the A609.

The Whittingehame Yew

One of Scotland's most famous and remarkable yew trees (*Taxus baccata*) stands in the East Lothian estate of Whittingehame.

Legend has it that in 1566 a dark deed was plotted in the sepulchral shade of this ancient yew – the murder of Mary, Queen of Scots' second husband, Lord Darnley. The conspirators included Lord Morton, resident in nearby Whittingehame Castle, and the Earl of Bothwell, Mary's lover and third husband-to-be. Darnley met his untimely end in 1567 when his Edinburgh lodgings were blown up.[1] The yew remains forever linked with this event in Scottish history.

The tree as it appeared in Elwes & Henrys' "The Trees of Great Britain and Ireland" in 1906.

This tree is one of Scotland's "layering" yews, its ever-increasing ring of outer growth covering a vast area of ground, radiating with perfect symmetry from a single, central trunk. Its dense canopy of graceful branches and dark foliage sweep to the ground, where they take root and layer. This forms a spacious inner sanctum which can only be accessed by a low entry tunnel through the outer ring of foliage.

Its relatively small trunk, measuring 3.64 metres (12 feet) in girth, belies the tree's great age. Historical measurements indicate a very slow rate of growth, with an increase of only 0.4 metres (1 foot 4 inches) in girth over the past 110 years, so that this yew might well be as much as 1000 years old.

Near Whittingehame Tower, near East Linton, East Lothian. Access is available only by prior permission.

The view outwards
from the centre of
the tree shows the
layering boughs.

The Whittingehame Eucalyptus

The Whittingehame Eucalyptus (*Eucalyptus whittingehamensis*) was raised from seed collected by the late Marquess of Salisbury in Tasmania. This impressive tree was planted about 160 years ago at Whittingehame, in East Lothian. It was realised that the tree wasn't the standard *Eucalyptus gunnii* and the famous 19th century tree enthusiasts, Elwes and Henry, became involved in a detailed study of it. Their conclusion was that the Whittingehame tree is a hybrid, with *E. gunnii* as one of the parents.

By 1904, the tree had already reached 18 to 19 metres (60 to 63 feet) tall and 4 metres (13 feet 5 inches) in girth at 0.6 metres (2 feet) above the ground.

Interestingly, Donald Rodger measured the tree 101 years later, in May 2005, and found that its girth is still the same, although his measurement was taken 1.5 metres (4 feet 6 inches) above the ground. However, the tree has grown to 25 metres (83 feet) tall.

During the severe winter of 1894 – 1895, the head gardener of the estate lost all the other Eucalyptuses growing on the estate. However, he discovered that none of the seedlings of *E. Whittingehamensis* were in the least injured, so he distributed them widely across the United Kingdom. Trees were grown from these seedlings in places as far apart as Kew Gardens in London, Blackmoor in Hampshire, Leonardslee in Sussex, Hatfield House in Hertfordshire, Sandhurst in Berkshire, and Abbotsbury in Dorset.

Near Whittingehame Tower, near East Linton, East Lothian. Access is available only by prior permission.

Act of Union Beeches

Clinging to the windswept slopes of North Berwick Law is a gaunt group of beech trees (*Fagus sylvatica*), planted to commemorate the Act of Union between the Scottish and English Parliaments in 1707. The local laird, Sir Hew Dalrymple, was one of the signatories to the Act.

The original planting comprised a small woodland, but all that remains is a group of eight bedraggled trees. Given their harsh growing environment, the trees have attained a respectable size, the tallest standing 31.2 metres (102 feet) high and the largest girth measuring 3.23 metres (10 feet 7 inches). Their thin, smooth bark has been wind-blasted to a silvery whiteness.

The eastern slopes of North Berwick Law, a hill immediately south of North Berwick, East Lothian. Sign-posted public car parking is available, and well-defined footpaths lead to the trees. Free public access is available all year.

The Newbattle Abbey Sycamore

To the front of Newbattle
Abbey, Dalkeith, Midlothian.
The abbey now functions as
an adult residential college.
Access with permission only.

This fine sycamore (*Acer pseudoplatanus*) grows in the grounds of Newbattle Abbey, on the outskirts of Dalkeith. It is reputed to be the oldest example of the species in Scotland, and perhaps in the United Kingdom. Thought to have been planted about 1550, it is an imposing tree, dominating the front of the house.

In 1904 the tree was recorded as being in good health with a full, billowing crown. It had then reached a height of 30 metres (98 feet) and its trunk measured 4.9 metres (16 feet) in girth. [1] However, it is now showing signs of age and natural decline, and the crown is becoming noticeably stag-headed. When measured in 2003, its height had reduced to 25 metres (82 feet) and the trunk had only gained an extra 60 centimetres (2 feet) in girth.

Many of the oldest and largest sycamores in the UK can be found in the grounds of country houses in Scotland. Originally known as plane, sycamore was probably brought to Scotland directly from France during the time of the Reformation in the mid-16th century. [1] Suited to the Scottish climate and soils, it soon became a common feature of the woodland and parkland on many estates. This Auld Alliance between the two countries has certainly left a rich legacy of wonderful trees.

As this book was going to press, disaster befell this celebrated tree, just a few days after inspection by tree surgeons, following concern about the tree's condition. On the 11th May, at 5pm, a freak gust of wind from the north blew the tree down across the main drive (see page 22). Fortunately, nobody was underneath.

The Dalkeith Park Oaks

A large group of veteran oak trees (*Quercus robur*) grows in the grounds of Dalkeith Palace, formerly a deer park. According to annual ring counts, most of the trees date from between 1580 and 1617, although some of them might have been planted as early as the 14th century. They display huge, multi-stemmed trunks, indicating that they have been coppiced early in their lives. The largest bases reach almost 10 metres (33 feet) in girth. [1]

This collection of oaks presents a rare landscape feature and a habitat of national importance, home to many endangered species of invertebrates. Veteran trees are vital elements of woodland ecosystems and have tremendous nature conservation value.

Parkland north of Dalkeith Palace, Midlothian. The estate is owned by the Duke of Buccleuch and the grounds are managed as a country park. Public access is available.

Stevenson's Yew

The famous Scottish author, Robert Louis Stevenson, spent part of his childhood with his maternal grandfather at Colinton Manse, Edinburgh. He is known to have played in the spreading branches of the old yew tree (*Taxus baccata*) in the garden. The remains of his swing are still evident on one of the limbs. Stevenson fondly recalls his early days at the manse in the company of the ancient tree:

> "*A yew, which is one of the glories of the village. Under the circuit of its wide, black branches, it was always dark and cool, and there was a green scurf over all the trunk among which glistened the round, bright drops of resin.*" [1]

The tree also provided inspiration for his poetry:

> "*Below the yew – it still is there –*
> *Our phantom voices haunt the air*
> *As we were still at play,*
> *And I can hear them call and say,*
> *'How far is it to Babylon?'*" [2]

R L Stevenson, aged 39
(1850 – 1894)

The tree is thought to be several centuries old and is recorded in the Kirk Session minutes of 1630. It is a fine specimen, with the trunk measuring 3.6 metres (12 feet) in girth. Despite losing some of its lower branches, the yew still stands today, a living link with one of Scotland's great literary figures.

The private garden of Colinton Manse, Dell Road, Edinburgh.
Access with permission.

Off the A902, about 1.6 kilometres (1 mile) north of Edinburgh city centre, with entrances at Inverleith Row (East Gate) and Arboretum Place (West Gate). Although entry to the Garden is free, there is a charge to enter the Glasshouses from Easter. The gardens are open daily (excluding 25 December and 1 January) from 10am.

The Royal Botanic Garden Silver Birch

Deserving a separate book to themselves, the National Botanic Gardens of Scotland (Edinburgh, Benmore, Dawyck and Logan) contain some of the nation's greatest heritage trees (see the Benmore Redwood Avenue page 179 and the Dawyck Silver Fir, Larch and Beech pages 40-43). Situated at Inverleith, Edinburgh, the Royal Botanic Garden Edinburgh hosts many fine heritage trees.

Several of these special trees now bear plaques under a recent "tree adoption" scheme, commemorating departed friends or relatives. They are often personal favourites, and regular visitors derive much pleasure from seeing "their" heritage tree growing through the seasonal cycle from bud burst to leaf fall.

One such specimen with a distinctive character is the fantastically contorted silver birch (*Betula pendula tristis*) beside the Caledonian Hall at the eastern end of the Garden. In the wild, silver birch die young, rarely living beyond 80 years. This mature example, planted sometime during the 19th century, is one of the oldest, largest and most beautiful birch trees in Scotland.

The Botanic Garden runs a Scottish Trees education programme. Children taking part can write their wishes on strips of cloth, which can be seen tied to the myriad of hanging branches – a continuation of the ancient "cloutie tree" tradition found in various parts of Scotland.

The Comiston House Austrian Pine

Austrian pines (*Pinus nigra* var. *nigra*) were first introduced to Britain by Messrs Lawson and Son, Edinburgh nurserymen, in 1835. This specimen was one of the first planted in the United Kingdom, in the grounds of Comiston House, built in 1815 by James Forrest, a prominent Edinburgh citizen of the time, and Lord Provost of the city from 1837 to 1843.

The tree was originally planted as part of an avenue which approached the house from the east. This avenue is now Camus Avenue, and during the latter half of the 20th century most of the remaining old trees from the avenue were felled during construction of a housing estate.

The remaining Austrian pine was condemned as unsafe during the construction works in 1990 because of its forked shape, but local residents who formed the Friends of Comiston Estate combined to try to save it. They engaged the help of Dr Page of the Royal Botanic Garden Edinburgh, whose comments on the tree ensured that the road layout was altered to allow the pine to remain.

The Fairmilehead Association (as the Friends of Comiston Estate is now known) has since adopted the tree's distinctive forked shape as its logo.

Other Austrian pines can also be seen at the nearby Oxgangs Police Station, which was originally Oxgangs Farmhouse and was part of the Estate of Comiston.

The tree stands in the front garden of No. 64, Camus Avenue, in the Comiston area of Edinburgh. It can readily be viewed at all times from the public footpath.

The Corstorphine Sycamore

For centuries, the Corstorphine Sycamore was one of Edinburgh's finest living landmarks. Its bright yellow foliage, which flushes several weeks earlier than is normal for the species, marks it out as unusual. It has been recognised as a distinct botanical variety and named *Acer pseudoplatanus* 'Corstorphinense', or Corstorphine sycamore, in recognition of its origin in the Edinburgh suburb.

The sycamore is thought to have been planted about 1600, and is steeped in local history and tradition. It is likely that it is a relict of a 16th century avenue of trees that led to Corstorphine Castle.

The shattered stump of the original tree.

In 1679 the second Lord Forrester, James Baillie, a drunk who engaged in several extra-marital relationships, was murdered by his lover, Cristian Nimmo, beneath the tree. She killed him with his own sword during a violent quarrel.

Another historical record notes that Lord Forrester is reputed to have buried treasure beneath the tree (please don't do any digging when you visit!), and villagers have been frightened off by a ghostly voice warning them to stop digging.

At its peak this ancient tree was almost 16.7 metres (55 feet) high and 3.8 metres (12 feet 6 inches) in girth. In 1955 the City of Edinburgh Council placed it under a Tree Preservation Order for its protection. The tree and the ground around it were gifted to The Corstorphine Trust in 1970.

Tragically, the tree was reduced to a shattered stump when it was blown down at 8.10pm in the Boxing Day gale of 1998. However, the ancient tree continued to survive until 2005, when it finally succumbed. Despite the unfortunate loss of Corstorphine's famous and much-loved landmark, it continues to live on in a number of artefacts made from the salvaged timber. The most notable is a beautiful violin, made by renowned maker Colin Adamson. It was commissioned by an anonymous benefactor on behalf of the Corstorphine Trust and donated to St Mary's Music School in Edinburgh, to be played by gifted musicians. This splendid instrument should provide pleasure for many years to come. Turned bowls, eggcups and clocks were also made from the timber.

Unfortunately, this tree did not produce seeds and could only be propagated from cuttings, from which other trees – its descendants – have been planted around Edinburgh.

> *A private garden on Dovecot Road, near its junction with Saughton Road North, in Corstorphine, a suburb of Edinburgh. Access is available only with permission.*

This fine example of Corstorphine sycamore stands at the gateway to Corstorphine churchyard, not far from the original tree.
Beautiful bowls turned from the wood of the fallen tree.
Amy Fields, from Caithness, a pupil of St Mary's Music School, plays the Corstorphine violin.

The Four Disciples

H uddled together in Malleny Garden on the outskirts of Edinburgh, stand four clipped yews (*Taxus baccata*), affectionately known as the Four Disciples. They are the sole survivors of a group of 12 trees, said to represent Christ's disciples. Unfortunately, eight were felled by a previous owner of the property as recently as 1961, which serves to highlight the ever-present threat to many of our important heritage trees. The garden and its remaining "disciples" are now in the care of the National Trust for Scotland. Nearby Malleny House was built for Sir James Murray in 1635, and the 12 Disciples were probably planted about that time.

The walled garden at Malleny Garden, sign-posted on the eastern edge of Balerno, a suburb of Edinburgh. Malleny Garden is owned by the National Trust for Scotland and is open to the public.

The Hopetoun House Morinda Spruce

The elegant Morinda spruce (*Picea smithiana*) grows naturally in the mountains of Nepal, Kashmir and Afghanistan. In 1818, some cones were sent by Dr George Govan, superintendent of Saharanpur, one of the oldest botanical gardens in India, to his father in Cupar, Fife. In turn, Dr Govan senior gave the cones to the Earl of Hopetoun, whose head gardener, James Smith, carefully germinated some seeds later that same year. These seedlings were kept in pots for three or four years, when two were planted out in the walled kitchen garden at Hopetoun. Others were grafted as cuttings on to Norway spruce rootstock, and planted in the gardens west of the house in 1826.

By the turn of this century, the taller spruce had reached a respectable 3.35 metres (11 feet) in girth and a height of 27.4 metres (90 feet). Sadly, one of the early root graft specimens severed at the grafted point of weakness when it succumbed to the gales of 2003. Its fallen carcass lies there still, a reminder of the risks facing such giants. Other root-grafted specimens are located in the tree collection close to Hopetoun House.

Originally known as the "Weeping fir" because of its long needles and pendulous branches, the Morinda is one of the beauties of the spruce world. That Hopetoun estate is home to the original Scottish plantings, and that Hopetoun's head gardener is remembered in the spruce's botanical name, is a fitting testimony to the Scottish link in the pedigree of this rare and attractive tree.

Within the tree collection 400 metres (440 yards)south west of Hopetoun House. Just south of the Forth Road Bridge, take the A904. Just under 1 kilometre (half a mile) along this road, turn right into South Queensferry. Directly under the road bridge there is a sign to Hopetoun House. The house and grounds are open daily from mid-April to mid-September, 11am - 5.30pm (last entry 4.30pm). Admission charges apply.

The Carnegie Tree

Andrew Carnegie
(1835 - 1919)

Andrew Carnegie's life is a classic tale of rags to riches. Born in Dunfermline in 1835 to a humble weaver, he emigrated with his family to the United States in 1848 in search of a better life. The entrepreneurial Carnegie worked hard through a succession of jobs, eventually starting his own steel company in Pittsburgh, Pennsylvania, in 1865. Such was the success of this that by the time he sold it in 1900 he was a multi-millionaire and one of the richest men in the world at the time. He became a firm believer in the "Gospel of Wealth": that wealthy individuals were morally obliged to give back to society, and devoted his later life to philanthropy and gave away a large proportion of his fortune to good causes. Carnegie never forgot the town of his birth, and one of his first gifts was to buy Pittencrieff Park, on the western edge of Dunfermline, in 1902. It had previously been a very private estate, and Carnegie was determined to provide an amenity that could be enjoyed by the local inhabitants, and particularly children.

Shortly after buying Pittencrieff Park, Carnegie planted an oak tree (*Quercus robur*) to commemorate the opening. A small plaque at the base of the tree records that it was planted on 18th May 1904. Carnegie was to plant many commemorative trees in his lifetime, but it is perhaps the fine oak which stands in his native town which is the most poignant. The tree is thriving and has reached impressive dimensions over the last century of growth, with a trunk girth of 2.71 metres (8 feet 11 inches), and a height of 19.6 metres (64 feet 4 inches). Carnegie's wife, Louise, planted an ash nearby.

After a long and illustrious life, Carnegie died in Massachusetts in 1919, one of the world's most famous and respected philanthropists.

Pittencrieff Park is on the western edge of the town of Dunfermline, Fife. Owned and managed by Fife Council, there is free public access throughout the year. Parking and access is available off the A907 Pittencrieff Street. The tree stands immediately to the east of the Glen Pavilion, close to an old locomotive on display.

The Cockairnie Sweet Chestnut

The sweet chestnut (*Castanea sativa*) at Cockairnie House, near Aberdour, Fife, holds the honour of being the largest-girthed example of its species in Scotland. It has a remarkable girth of 8.82 metres (29 feet), and it would take six fully grown adults with outstretched arms linked together to encircle the trunk. Cockairnie House is about 500 years old, and the tree was probably planted shortly after the house was built.

The tree has a vast, pot-bellied trunk that appears to consist of one huge burr around its entire circumference. This natural growth deformity undoubtedly exaggerates its girth.

The private garden of Cockcairnie House, about 3.2 kilometres (2 miles) west of Aberdour, Fife. Access is available only with permission.

Lady Miller's Beech

The fine, open-grown beech (*Fagus sylvatica*) which stands next to the old coach road between Auchtermuchty and Perth is known as Lady Miller's Beech. "Lady Miller" ran a tavern at Broomhall, and was renowned for the illicit still she operated from a nearby cave, using the pure water of a natural well. Her hospitality was acclaimed by drovers and travellers, and her illegal spirits were regularly smuggled into Perth. Nothing now survives of the inn, but the solitary beech tree stands as a living memorial to this colourful character. [1] Its trunk measures 3.39 metres (11 feet 2 inches) in girth, and its windswept crown is 19.3 metres (63 feet 4 inches) tall.

Alongside a minor road midway between Auchtermuchty and Perth, close to Broomhall. The site is managed by Forestry Commission Scotland and there is public access at all times.

The Balmerino
Sweet Chestnut

The peaceful ruins of Balmerino Abbey lie on the rural coast of north Fife. In the grounds of the abbey grows an ancient sweet chestnut (*Castanea sativa*), remarkable for its size and form. Its massive trunk, with characteristically twisted grain, displays huge, bulbous swellings, and its two main limbs almost appear to wrap around each other. Although it is certainly of great age, the tree is in remarkably good condition and continues to thrive.

This sweet chestnut also has an intriguing royal provenance, because it has been closely linked to two Scottish queens. One tradition claims that it was planted by Queen Ermengarde at the foundation of the abbey in 1229. A more plausible explanation is that it was planted by Mary, Queen of Scots in 1565 during a two-day visit to the Abbey. Tests carried out by the National Trust for Scotland in 1979 confirmed the tree to be between 390 and 425 years old, adding credence to this claim.

If it was indeed planted by Mary in 1565, it would be the second-oldest sweet chestnut in the United Kingdom with a known planting date, the oldest being at Castle Leod (see 1550 Chestnut, page 238).

An Edwardian postcard of the tree.

The grounds of Balmerino Abbey, Balmerino, about 4.8 kilometres (3 miles) west of Newport-on-Tay, Fife, on the southern shore of the Firth of Tay. The abbey is owned by the National Trust for Scotland and access is available throughout the year. There is an honesty box for donations.

St Andrews Holm Oak and Queen Mary's Thorn

Two of Scotland's Heritage Trees grace the quadrant of St Mary's College, St Andrews University. One is a holm oak (*Quercus ilex*), a species introduced to the United Kingdom about 1500, and of which there are only a few good examples in Scotland. This fine, open-grown specimen continues to thrive. Thought to have been planted about 1740, its short trunk measures 3.67 metres (12 feet) in girth, the largest recorded for this species in Scotland. The stately tree forms a striking central feature within this ancient seat of learning.

The ancient hawthorn (*Crataegus monogyna*) that also graces the quadrant is reputed to have been planted in 1563 by Mary, Queen of Scots, during one of her many visits to the town. This small tree certainly possesses character and an air of importance, sitting as it does at the heart of a famous seat of learning and having a royal provenance.

All that remains of the original tree is a decayed stump that is disintegrating badly. Judging by the size of this remnant, the tree must have had a considerable girth for its species. However, this veteran is still alive, three relatively young stems arising phoenix-style from the base of the old stump, to form a full and healthy crown. This living link with one of Scotland's most famous historical figures thus continues to survive, producing new and vigorous growth from the shattered hulk of the original tree.

The quadrant of St Mary's College, St Andrews University,
St Andrews, Fife. Public access is available off the main street.

The Bogle Bush

It is said in the Perthshire village of Kinrossie that if anything happens to the Bogle Bush, the village will suffer. This large sycamore (*Acer pseudoplatanus*) stands beside the road from Kinrossie to the Saucher crossroads and, indeed, it actually encroaches into the road. This means that passing cars and vehicles have to manoeuvre around the tree, leading to concern in the village about the damage that might be caused to it by passing buses.

In 2000 a local councillor said of the tree that it "encroaches on to the road and it only has to get clipped by a harvester or a bus and it could get badly damaged. We want to make sure that if that happens, it doesn't get condemned."

The health of this tree has concerned the villagers for many years, because there are old metal bands placed into the tree about 10 feet up, to hold it together. These bands have served their purpose, but now, ironically, are beginning to cut into the bark of the tree, because they haven't been slackened. However, despite the bands and the risks of the passing traffic, the tree is still in good health, which can only be to the good of the village.

The origin of the tree's unusual name is obscure. It may derive from 'Bogle-about-the-Bush', an old Scot's phrase for the childhood game of 'hide-and-seek', or it may possibly be linked to sightings of ghosts and apparitions.

The tree stands just east of Kinrossie, in Perth & Kinross, on the north side of the road on the way to the Saucher crossroads.

Cromwell's Tree

At first glance this ancient sweet chestnut (*Castanea sativa*) looks all but dead, but although the upper parts of the tree are a mass of dead, bleached, bare branches, the lower half is still alive and thriving.

Growing in a field near the town of Bridge of Earn, the tree is surrounded by coloured glass fragments and clinker from an earlier industrial use of the site. This ancient, strangely beautiful tree commemorates the fact that Oliver Cromwell set up camp in Bridge of Earn in 1651, before he marched on nearby Perth. Although old enough to have been present when Cromwell was in town, whether there is in fact a direct relationship between the two is, unfortunately, lost in the mists of time.

Growing in a field, south-west of Bridge of Earn, Perth & Kinross. Travel south from the village and cross over the railway bridge. The tree is in the centre of the field just south of the railway. An informal footpath leads to it.

King James VI Sycamore

The strong connections between Scone Palace and royalty are reflected in the many commemorative trees that grace the well-kept gardens and grounds, a tradition continued to this day. One of the finest is the huge old sycamore (*Acer pseudoplatanus*) reputed to have been planted by King James VI of Scotland and I of England in 1617, during his long-awaited "hame-coming". This was his only visit to his homeland following the Union of the Scottish and English Crowns in 1603. James also planted an oak, which still survives.

The sycamore is a majestic specimen. Four huge limbs emerge from the short, squat trunk at between 2 metres and 3 metres (6 feet 6 inches and 10 feet) from ground level to form a vast, spreading canopy of good shape. Its trunk measures 5.5 metres (18 feet) in girth at 0.3 metres (1 foot) below large swellings where the main limbs arise, and it is 21.3 metres (70 feet) tall. In 1883 its girth was recorded at 3.64 metres (12 feet) at 1.2 metres (4 feet) above the ground, and its height at 24.4 metres (80 feet). [1] The loss of one of the main limbs in a storm in 2002 has left the tree somewhat unbalanced.

A wood engraving of Scone Palace in 1823 by J P Neale. One of the trees to the right of the building may well be the King James VI Sycamore.

On the terrace close to the south east corner of Scone Palace, on the A93 road a short distance north of Perth, Perth & Kinross. The house and grounds are usually open from Good Friday to mid-October, and admission charges apply. Tours are available in winter by prior appointment with the estate office.

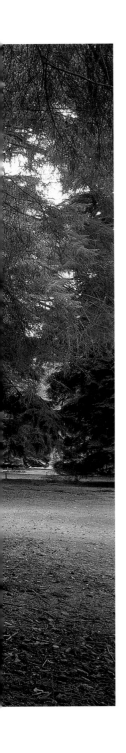

Scone's Sitkas

Scone Estate, in Perthshire, boasts four remarkable Sitka spruce (*Picea sitchensis*) trees notable for their huge size and uniformity of appearance. These were planted in 1848 and form part of the impressive pinetum which was to be established over the succeeding four years. Each tree occupies the corner of a rectangle measuring 74 by 24 metres (81 by 26 yards) in a formal design which is reflected in the series of avenues which characterise the pinetum.

Notwithstanding their relatively tender years, they tower more than 50 metres (164 feet) and their mighty trunks range in girth from 6.4 to 7.4 metres (20 feet 10 inches to 24 feet 4 inches). The girth of the trunks is exaggerated by the particularly flared, moss-covered buttress roots, a feature which has led to marked discrepancies in their measurements over the years.

All four trees exhibit perfectly straight trunks which taper imperceptibly towards the tip of the leading shoot, and they are enshrouded within impeccably conical crowns of dark foliage almost extending to ground level. The trees stand like silent, living monoliths of the arboricultural world.

The pinetum at Scone contains an exceptional collection of very large trees, including many fine western hemlock, noble fir, and giant sequoia laid out in regular avenues. With such a dizzying concentration of arboricultural giants, it is all too easy to lose perspective of height and scale and feel humbled in their presence.

> At the rear of the pinetum, near the perimeter fence, in the grounds of Scone Palace, near Scone, Perth & Kinross, a short distance north of Perth on the A93 road to Braemar. The house and grounds are normally open from Good Friday to mid-October and admission charges apply. Tours are available in winter by prior appointment with the estate office.

David Douglas
(1799 - 1834)

This magnificent tree was grown from seed brought back from the Pacific north west of North America by celebrated Scottish botanist and explorer David Douglas – hence its name. Most likely the seed was collected in 1825 from the lower reaches of the Columbia River, near Fort Vancouver, arriving in Britain in 1827. The seeds were sown, the seedlings raised in a nursery, and then planted out at Scone in 1834, the year that Douglas was killed on the slopes of Mauna Kea, Hawaii, when he fell into a wild cattle trap. He is buried at Kawaiahoa Church, Honolulu. Renowned botanist H J Elwes said that "the tree was transplanted to its current position in 1850". [1]

Douglas was born within the grounds of Scone Palace and worked there as a gardener. In 1820 he was accepted for a post at the Botanic Gardens, Glasgow, under Dr William Hooker, and he began his plant-hunting expeditions in 1823. Among his other discoveries are the noble and grand firs and the Sitka spruce, now the United Kingdom's most important timber tree.

Grown from the first seed to arrive in Britain and planted close to his birthplace, this Douglas fir (*Pseudotsuga menziesii*) is a living memorial to a great plant hunter whose discoveries shaped much of the commercial forest landscape of Britain.

> *Next to the ruins of the old village of Scone, Perth & Kinross, in the grounds of Scone Palace, a short distance north of Perth on the A93 road to Braemar. The house and grounds are normally open from Good Friday to mid-October and admission charges apply. Tours are available in winter by prior appointment with the estate office.*

The Scone Douglas Fir

The King of the Forest

Standing majestically on the northern edge of Muirward Wood, near New Scone, Perthshire, the monolithic Scots pine (*Pinus sylvestris*) known as the King of the Forest lives up to its regal title.

With a girth of 6.09 metres (20 feet), this pine boasts the largest trunk recorded for this species in the United Kingdom. Its vertical growth is equally impressive at 31 metres (102 feet). Towering above the surrounding plantation, this mighty named tree is an outstanding example of Scotland's native pine.

The tree forks into three trunks of roughly equal size at two metres (6 feet 6 inches) above ground level. These rise skywards almost parallel with each other to form a single canopy of good shape. Its lower branches have been suppressed and have died off early in the life of the tree, the pinkish hue of the deeply fissured bark being clearly visible today.

The tree was already regarded as a novelty in the late 19th century. In 1883 it was recorded as being about 300 years old, 24.4 metres (80 feet) tall and 4.88 metres (16 feet) in girth. [1] At that time its triumvirate of huge trunks was calculated to contain 11.3 cubic metres (400 cubic feet) of timber.

Muirward Wood, about 3.2 kilometres (2 miles) north of New Scone, Perth & Kinross. The tree is very difficult to find amidst a maze of forest tracks. Public access is available via footpaths from New Scone.

*The private grounds
of Methven Castle,
off the A85 road
about 1.6 kilometres
(1 mile) east of
Methven, Perth &
Kinross. Access is
available only with
permission.*

The Pepperwell Oak

This celebrated English or pedunculate oak tree (*Quercus robur*) stands in the private grounds of Methven Castle, Perthshire. Taking its unusual name from a nearby spring, it is an imposing specimen with a girth of 7.16 metres (23 feet 6 inches) and a height of 23.8 metres (78 feet). Several centuries old, this tree has been well known in the area since the 18th century. In 1722 the princely sum of 100 Scottish merks was offered for the tree. The oak was also described as being of "great picturesque beauty" in 1837, and "…in every respect a noble specimen of the brave old oak" in 1883. [1] Tradition also reports that a stone lies at the centre of the trunk.

The Mother & Father Trees

D avid Douglas introduced the fir that bears his name to these shores in 1827 (see page 112). Only a handful of these first trees survive, including the Mother and Father Trees, at Lynedoch, Scone. This pair of Douglas fir (*Pseudotsuga menziesii*) supplied much of the early seed until about 1861 for plantings that helped to change the face of Scottish forestry. Such was the demand for their seed that between 1845 and 1853 the Lynedoch trees realised £500. [1] One tree measures 6.03 metres (19 feet 10 inches) in girth by 40 metres (131 feet) in height, and the other 6.15 metres (20 feet 3 inches) in girth and 48.5 metres (159 feet) in height.

Private woodland close to Lynedoch Cottage in the Almond Valley, part of Scone Estate, about 3.2 kilometres (2 miles) north of Methven, Perth & Kinross. The trees are difficult to locate and access is available only by permission.

Eppie Callum's Oak

A handsome oak in the Perthshire town of Crieff is known affectionately as Eppie Callum's Oak. Several centuries old, it is said to have played a role in Scotland's turbulent history, sheltering the outlaw Rob Roy Macgregor (1671 - 1734) and Bonnie Prince Charlie (1720 - 1788) from their enemies.

The tree takes its name from a local worthy who ran the Oakbank Inn, a favourite hostelry with cattle drovers from the Highlands. Records confirm that there was indeed an old crone named Eppie Callum resident in Crieff, although it would appear that she was born long after the oak is said to have taken root. Regardless of this historical discrepancy, Eppie's name remains associated with the tree to this day.

The inimitable Dundee poet, William McGonagall (1825 - 1902), mentioned the tree in his poem, "Beautiful Crieff":

> "Then there's Lady Mary's Walk near the Bridge of Turret,
> Which I hope visitors will go and see and not forget,
> Because nearby grows a magnificent oak most lovely to see,
> Which is known by the name of Eppie Callum's Tree."

Measuring 24 metres (79 feet) tall and with an impressive girth of 5.65 metres (18 feet 7 inches), this well known named tree is a prominent sight in the local street scene.

An Edwardian postcard showing the tree from behind with an adjacent building (no longer standing).

A private garden at the junction of Laggan Road and Turretbank Road, Crieff, Perth & Kinross. It can be readily viewed from the public road.

119

The Camperdown Elm

The Camperdown Elm (*Ulmus glabra* 'Camperdownii') is a natural mutant of Scotland's native wych elm. It was discovered by chance about 1835 growing wild in woodland by the Earl of Camperdown's head forester, David Taylor. Intrigued by its alien appearance, Taylor carefully lifted and transplanted the tree to the landscaped grounds which surround Camperdown House, on the outskirts of Dundee. Before long, interest in this outlandish variety grew and the Camperdown elm provided the early cuttings from which it was to be widely propagated. The instantly recognisable form of the tree soon became a common sight in parks, gardens and cemeteries.

The original tree survives to this day, and has so far escaped the ravages of Dutch elm disease. Standing no more than 3 metres (10 feet) tall, the weeping branches extend to the ground. However, it is the bizarre branch architecture that is its most remarkable feature. The crown consists of a mass of heavily convoluted and twisted branches knotted together in dense clusters. These painfully and impossibly double back repeatedly on one another to create a marvellous living sculpture unrivalled by any other variety of tree.

Camperdown Park, on the north western outskirts of Dundee. It is owned and managed by Dundee City Council, and free public access is available at all times.

The Dibble Tree

Tammas Lowson's Dibble, Carnoustie

This quaint title belongs to a willow (*Salix alba* 'caerulea') growing near the centre of Carnoustie, Angus. A tree of great local significance, it is said to have originated from a "dibble", or planting stick, absent-mindedly left in the ground in 1797 by Tammas Lousen (Thomas Lowson), an itinerant shipwright and salmon fisher. As the tree took root and began to grow, he decided to settle down and build a house. Others came to join him, and soon this solitary willow tree became a symbol of their community. From its humble beginning as a small, coastal crofting community, Carnoustie grew into the popular holiday and golfing resort it is today. The willow tree still stands, a living tribute to the town's founding father.

The tree is of no great size for its reputed age, with a girth of only 1.73 metres (5 feet 8 inches) and a height of 10.5 metres (34 feet). The elements have not been kind, and the tree was apparently split in two by a lightning strike in the mid-18th century. However, regular pruning has maintained a healthy flush of foliage each year.

The tree was restored by Angus Council as part of the Burgh's bicentennial celebrations in 1997.

Edwardian postcard revealing how little the tree has grown in the last century.

Next to the public toilets on a small lane off Ferrier Street, 50 metres (55 yards) south of the town centre of Carnoustie, Angus. It is well signposted. Free public access is available throughout the year.

House of Dun Redwoods

The House of Dun is a small but handsome Georgian mansion built to a William Adam design in 1730. Close to the coastal Angus town of Montrose, it enjoys commanding views over the Montrose Basin. By far the most notable landscape feature is the line of 16 giant sequoia (*Sequoiadendron giganteum*) trees which dominate the skyline. Not only do these provide an impressive setting for the house, but such is their prominence in the landscape that apparently modern-day mariners use them as a navigational aid.

The trees are reputed to be some of the earliest examples of the species in Scotland, having been planted only two years after it was introduced in 1853. They are handsome specimens which appear to be able to tolerate the rather exposed, coastal conditions, and are remarkably uniform in appearance. One of the largest trees measures 7 metres (23 feet) in girth and 37 metres (121 feet) in height, although the tallest has attained a respectable 39 metres (128 feet).

The House of Dun is on the A935, 4.8 kilometres (3 miles) west of Montrose, Angus. It is a property of the National Trust for Scotland and is well sign-posted. The grounds are open throughout the year. Admission charges apply.

Old
Maggie

Belmont Castle lies approximately
0.8 kilometres (0.5 miles) south of
the Perthshire village of Meigle.
Sign-posted access is off the B954.
The beech stands on the lawns to
the front of the castle. The castle
and its grounds are owned by
Dundee City Council and leased to
Church of Scotland, which has run
the castle as an eventide home since
1931. Access with permission.

Belmont Castle, near Meigle in Perthshire, was formerly the home of Sir Henry Campbell-Bannerman, Liberal Prime Minister from 1905 to 1908. Born in Glasgow in 1836, he enjoyed a long and distinguished political career, serving as MP for the Stirling Burghs from 1868. He became Prime Minister at the relatively late age of 69, and having retired due to ill health, died at 10 Downing Street within 18 days of giving up office. He is buried in Meigle Parish Churchyard, close to his beloved castle.

It was Sir Henry who gave the name "Old Maggie" to the fine copper beech (*Fagus sylvatica* 'purpurea') which stands on the lawn to the front of Belmont Castle. The tree was a particular favourite of his and it is said that he used to sit under its dark and sombre shade to think and discuss affairs of state. He apparently enjoyed the peace and tranquillity of the old tree, a far cry from the hustle and bustle of Whitehall. Quite why Sir Henry called it "Old Maggie", no one knows. However the affectionate nickname has stuck to this day and the beech has become forever associated with one of the UK's Prime Ministers.

The beech tree is indeed a fine, open-grown specimen which forms a striking focal point on the lawn. The short, squat trunk supports a full, spreading crown, and the foliage is of a particularly dark and uniform purple. The trunk measures 5.0 metres (16 feet 5 inches) in girth at its narrowest point 0.5 metres (1 foot 7 inches) above ground level, and the shapely canopy reaches 25 metres (82 feet) in height.

In the bad old days of rough justice and summary execution, certain trees were commonly pressed into service as informal gibbets, on which wrong-doers met their gruesome ends (see also the "dool" trees at Blairquhan and Leith Hall, pp 34 and 220). One such gallows tree survives near the village of Monikie in Angus. Here, a large, solitary beech (*Fagus sylvatica*) with a dark and grisly history stands atop Gallows Hill, a low, rounded eminence just over 200 metres (656 feet) high which commands panoramic views over the surrounding countryside. The boughs of this tree are believed to have been used for hanging law-breakers.

It is easy to see why the beech was chosen as a gallows. Standing as it does at the summit of a hill, the crown has been swept to the east by the prevailing winds to create a very imbalanced and one-sided structure, with several large, long limbs orientated almost parallel to the ground. The latter are ideal for attaching a noose and, with at least eight metres between the lowest limb and the ground, make for a good clean "drop". The tree's prominent location in the landscape would also have meant that the unfortunate victim must have been visible for miles around, acting as a deterrent to would-be criminals.

The tree is still in good health, despite its very exposed and inhospitable location. It is short and sturdy in appearance and stands no more than 15.7 metres (51 feet) tall. The single, clean trunk has an impressive girth of 4.42 metres (14 feet 6 inches), and bears the scars of numerous old engravings, most now illegible. It is a sobering experience to stand under the grim natural scaffold of this isolated old landmark and reflect on what macabre events it was unwittingly party to.

The gallows tree is located on the summit of Gallows Hill, approximately 1.6 kilometres (1 mile) north of the village of Monikie, Angus. Follow the B978 north from Dundee for approximately 11.2 kilometres (7 miles). Turn off at the sign-post for the Douglaswood Scout Centre and follow the rough track for 400 metres (quarter of a mile). Park at the gates to the Scout centre and walk along the south side of the security fence for approximately 400 metres (440 yards). (The ground is rough here, and the path poorly defined). At a World War II pillbox, move inside the fence and follow a track through woodland uphill for approximately 200 metres (218 yards). The single, isolated beech stands at the top of the hill, on the edge of the pine plantation.

The Gallows Tree

Pitmuies Sweet Chestnut

This fine sweet chestnut (*Castanea sativa*) stands in pride of place on the lawns to the front of the House of Pitmuies, in the rolling Angus countryside. The house is a fine, classically styled mansion which dates from 1730, although it incorporates an earlier dwelling of the 17th century. It sits within a designed landscape largely laid out between 1768 and 1820, and is renowned for its fine gardens extending to 10 hectares (25 acres) in total.

The sweet chestnut is undoubtedly a very large and fine specimen in excellent health despite its exposed position. The gnarled and burred trunk measures an impressive 7.62 metres (25 feet) in girth, making it one of the largest in Scotland, while the lofty canopy reaches 22 metres (72 feet) in height. The framework is formed of huge limbs, each in themselves the size of a decent tree, and the huge, billowing canopy is in good health. An old swing and other gymnastic equipment attached to the lower branches suggest that this tree was a popular attraction in times past. It is not known exactly when the tree was planted, but it is likely to be more than 300 years old and associated with the early development of the house and estate.

A smaller, though equally fine, sweet chestnut stands close by, and measures 5.05 metres (16 feet 7 inches) in girth and 20.8 metres (68 feet) in height.

Pitmuies House Garden is approximately 11.2 kilometres (7 miles) east of Forfar, near the village of Friockheim, Angus. It is clearly signposted off the A932 road. The gardens are open daily to the public from 1 April to 31 October. Admission charges apply.

Glamis Horse Chestnut

lamis Castle, the childhood home of the late Queen Elizabeth the Queen Mother, has been a royal residence since 1372. In front of the castle stands a fine, old horse chestnut (*Aesculus hippocastanum*), said to have been a favourite of the Queen Mother.

An open-grown specimen, it is recorded as being planted in 1746. It has large, heavy limbs that radiate from the short trunk and descend to the ground. The resulting ring of greenery forms a secluded enclosure. In 1884 the tree was already large, the trunk measuring 3.27 metres (9 feet 10 inches) in girth and 16.8 metres (55 feet) in height. By 1999, the girth had increased to 4.17 metres (13 feet 9 inches) and the height to 20.3 metres (67 feet).

The lawn in front of Glamis Castle, near Forfar, Angus. The castle is open to the public from April until October. Admission charges apply.

The Meikleour Beech Hedge

The impressive beech (*Fagus sylvatica*) hedge that runs alongside the busy A93 road has since 1966 been officially recognised as the tallest in the world. This over-powering "green wall" stands 36.6 metres (120 feet) tall at its northern end and gradually diminishes to a mere 24.2 metres (80 feet) at its southern extremity, with an average height of 30 metres (100 feet). About 530 metres (1738 feet) long, it is cut and re-measured every 10 years, a complex operation that takes four men about six weeks to complete.

An Edwardian postcard of the hedge.

The hedge is believed to have been laid out and planted in the autumn of 1745, the year of the second Jacobite uprising, by Jean Mercer and her husband, Robert Murray Nairne. Following the death of her husband at the battle of Culloden a year later, Jean Mercer moved to Edinburgh to live with friends, leaving the young hedge to grow untended. A more romantic version of events has it that the gardeners who planted the hedge took up arms for Bonnie Prince Charlie and perished on the field of Culloden. Their hedge was left to grow untended towards the heavens as a living monument to their memory.

Whatever the explanation for its great height, the hedge is now a world-beating wonder and a popular attraction for tourists.

Alongside the A93 trunk road about 6.4 kilometres (4 miles) south of Blairgowrie, Perth & Kinross. Parking and an interpretation board are available.

The Hermitage Douglas and the Dunkeld Douglas

A small woodland immediately west of Dunkeld Cathedral, Dunkeld, Perth & Kinross. Public access is available throughout the year via a footpath.

Standing not far from each other near the Perthshire village of Dunkeld are two of Scotland's most impressive Douglas firs. One is a sometime contender for the title of tallest tree in the United Kingdom, and the other has the largest girth of its species in the United Kingdom.

At a towering 59 metres (194 feet) tall, the graceful Douglas fir (*Pseudotsuga menziesii*) at the Hermitage, near Dunkeld, Perthshire, is one of the tallest trees in the UK. It nestles at the bottom of a steep gorge, with its roots in the turbulent River Braan. It is an elegant specimen, with a single, slender trunk and spire-shaped crown in perfect form to the tip of its leading shoot.

It is thought that the tree began life about 1875 as a self-sown seedling from the grove of older specimens on the opposite bank of the river. Its relatively young age makes its impressive vertical growth all the more remarkable.

Nearby, the Douglas with the champion girth stands next to Dunkeld Cathedral. Despite its impressive girth of 7 metres (23 feet), it is easily overlooked because it is located in woodland containing many fine trees of great size.

Said to have been planted as a gift to the Duke of Atholl about 1846, it is coarsely branched and not particularly attractive. Its top was blown out many years ago, and it now stands at just over 30 metres (98 feet) tall. The bark on the lower trunk is exceptionally thick and deeply fissured, a characteristic that undoubtedly contributes to its vast bulk.

On the south bank of the River Braan at the Hermitage, near Dunkeld, Perth & Kinross. The Hermitage is signposted off the A9 highway, and the tree is signposted and readily viewed from the National Trust for Scotland property on the north side of the river. The site is managed by Forestry Commission Scotland, and free public access is available throughout the year.

The Parent Larch

"DUNKELD LARCHES"

With a girth of 5.6 metres (18 feet 6 inches), this is one of the largest European larches (*Larix decidua*) in the United Kingdom. It was planted after a visit to Dunkeld by a "Mr Menzies of Megeny in Glenlyon, who in 1738 brought a few small larch plants in his portmanteau, five of which he left for Duke James of Atholl." Of those five, one was cut by the gardener about 1790 "by mistake", and two were felled in 1809. [1] The present tree is the last of the original five planted by Duke James. His successors, notably the 4th Duke (John, 1755 - 1830), known as the Planting Duke, were increasingly absorbed with planting European larch on the hills of the Atholl Estates. By 1830 the total planted by all the dukes exceeded 14 million larch trees covering nearly 4250 hectares (10,500 acres). [1]

This tree and its now dead companions had already been dubbed the "Parent Larches" by 1812 because they provided some of the seed for the early plantings. [2] The remaining tree now stands as a monument to the tree-planting feats achieved by the dukes and, although an old tree, it is still a magnificent specimen.

The Dunkeld Larches
by G W Wilson,
from *The Larch*
by C Y Michie (1882).

Alongside the footpath that runs west of the main (north) car park in Dunkeld, Perth & Kinross, and skirts the edge of Dunkeld Cathedral, where the path meets the woodland on the edge of the grounds of the Hilton Dunkeld House Hotel, 24 kilometres (15 miles) north of Perth. Free public access is available.

The Pedestal Larches

Only two examples of so-called "pedestal" larch are known to exist in Scotland. The prefix "pedestal" refers to the tree's shape when a perfectly normal-looking tree sits atop a vastly swollen and contorted base. The distinction between the normal tree and the base tends to be very obvious, giving the impression that the trunk is growing out of a raised pedestal. This phenomenon is very rare and only eight such larch trees are known within the United Kingdom.

The largest Scottish pedestal larch is a rather exposed and wind-battered specimen standing isolated in a field below Foswell House, near the Perthshire town of Auchterarder. The grossly distended and gnarled pedestal rises to a height of 1.2 metres (3 feet 11 inches) and has a massive girth of 8.96 metres (29 feet 5 inches) measured at 1 metre above ground, narrowing abruptly thereafter. This monstrous podium is in sharp contrast to the perfectly normal stem which sits atop it, with its much more modest girth at 2 metres (6 feet 6 inches) above ground of 5.03 metres (16 feet 6 inches). The trunk has a pronounced lean to the east, with a contorted crown bearing long, almost weeping, branches. If it was not for the relentless browsing by sheep, it is highly likely that these would touch the ground and layer.

The other Scottish example also resides in Perthshire, on a wooded hillside to the rear of the Dunkeld House Hotel. Although the pedestal is not as large as the Foswell tree, it is the better specimen of the two and provides an excellent example of this outlandish growth habit. The pedestal also stands at 1.2 metres (3 feet 11 inches) in height and has a girth of 7.88 metres (25 feet 10 inches). This narrows very abruptly and the "normal" trunk which emerges from it has the much reduced girth of 5.03 metres (16 feet 6 inches). The crown appears to be in good health and condition, although decay has set into the butt region.

In common with the other known pedestal larches in the UK, the swollen bases appear to consist of twisted and conglomerated masses of roots with a very distinct "root collar" where the normal trunk arises. One plausible theory as to how such trees arise is that they have been propagated in containers and retained within restricted growing environments for prolonged periods, with the result that they have become "pot bound" and the roots over-crowded and distorted. Once such trees were planted out, the growth pressures exerted by the downward spiral of the deformed root systems gradually forced the root balls out of the ground. The amalgamated mass of the exposed roots grow at a disproportionate rate to the trunks, thus creating the enlarged pedestals.

The trees are clearly of considerable age and are thought to date from around 1720 – 1740.

The Foswell Pedestal Larch stands in a field near Foswell House, approximately 1.6 kilometres (1 mile) on minor roads off the A9 to the south of Auchterarder, Perth & Kinross. The Dunkeld Pedestal Larch stands on the hillside immediately behind the Dunkeld House Hotel, Dunkeld, Perth & Kinross. Access is available with the permission of the hotel.

The Monzie Larch

This "champion" European larch (*Larix decidua*) has the largest girth so far recorded for its species in the United Kingdom. Situated at Monzie Castle, near Crieff, Perthshire, it boasts an impressive girth of 6.03 metres (19 feet 10 inches) and a height of 35 metres (115 feet). It might even be the largest-girthed of its type in the world, because only one other, in the Italian Tyrol, is reputed to be as big. [1]

The tree began as one of six seedlings brought from the Tyrol in 1737 by Colonel John Menzies of Glen Lyon, Perthshire. On his way to deliver the new species to the Duke of Atholl at Dunkeld, he broke his journey at Monzie Castle. Tradition says the larches were either stolen from his hamper, or were given to the Laird of Monzie in return for his hospitality. [2]

The Original Japanese Larches

The Japanese larch (*Larix kaempferi*) was introduced to Britain in 1861 by the Victorian plant collector, Henry Veitch. Twenty-six years later the 7th Duke of Atholl became interested in this new species. He brought seed from Japan and planted 14 trees near Dunkeld House in 1887. Eleven of these trees form a shallow crescent lining the driveway to this day.

The success of that planting was largely responsible for the Japanese larch's rise to prominence as one of Scotland's principal commercial forestry species. It is now widely planted as a timber tree, being able to resist larch canker, a serious disease of its European cousin (*Larix decidua*), and to grow rapidly over a wider range of site conditions than European larch can.

The Dunkeld trees are notable as the parents of the first hybrid larch (*Larix × eurolepis*), first recognised in 1904.

The trees form a shallow crescent on the north side of the private driveway serving Dunkeld House Hotel, Dunkeld, Perth & Kinross. Public access and an interpretation panel are available.

The Birnam Oak

William Shakespeare
(1564 – 1616)

An ancient sessile oak (*Quercus petraea*) standing on the banks of the River Tay near the Perthshire village of Birnam is said to be the last survivor of the legendary Birnam Wood, immortalised in Shakespeare's "Macbeth":

> *"Macbeth shall never vanquish'd be until*
> *Great Birnam Wood to high Dunsinane Hill*
> *Shall come against him."*

The witches' prophecy literally came true, when Malcolm's army camouflaged itself with branches from the great wood and took by surprise Macbeth's stronghold at Dunsinane, 20 kilometres (12 miles) to the south east:

> *"As I did stand my watch upon the hill,*
> *I looked toward Birnam and anon methought*
> *The wood began to move."*

The tragic Macbeth then meets his gruesome end.

On the south bank of the River Tay at Birnam, Perth & Kinross, accessible via a sign-posted footpath from Dunkeld bridge and another from the Birnam House Hotel in the centre of the village. Free public access is available throughout the year.

It is unlikely that this fine old veteran, sometimes known as "Macbeth's Oak", was around to furnish Malcolm's soldiers with greenery when the battle is reputed to have been fought, in 1057. It is, however, several centuries old and represents a living relic of the great medieval oakwood which once clothed the banks of the Tay.

The trunk boasts an impressive girth of 5.5 metres (18 feet) and a widely spreading canopy composed of long, horizontal limbs. A stately survivor of a bygone age, its literary connection has resulted in its becoming one of Scotland's better-known heritage trees.

The Birnam Sycamore

Almost as famous as its near neighbour, the Birnam Oak (see page 140), the mighty sycamore (*Acer pseudoplatanus*) growing on the fertile banks of the River Tay is an impressive sight. Thought to be more than 300 years old, it appears to be an out-grown pollard that now supports a huge, spreading, dome-shaped crown typical of the species. Particularly remarkable are its buttress roots, which seem to mould themselves to the bank of the river.

The tree's girth has frequently been measured over the years and shows steady and vigorous growth: 6.1 metres (20 feet) in 1906, 6.7 metres (22 feet) in 1956, 7.1 metres (23 feet 4 inches) in 1981 and 7.62 metres (25 feet) in 2006.

On the south bank of the River Tay at the village of Birnam, Perth & Kinross, reached via a sign-posted footpath from Dunkeld bridge and another from the Birnam House Hotel in the centre of the village. Free public access is available throughout the year.

Neil Gow's Oak

Neil Gow (1727 - 1807), a famous Scottish fiddler, is reputed to have composed many of Scotland's best-loved strathspeys and reels in the shade of this old sessile oak (*Quercus petraea*), which grows on the banks of the River Tay, near Dunkeld, Perthshire. The tree that now bears his name is also known as the "Fiddle Tree", and stands in living memory of this colourful character. The Gow family brought folk music into a new professional era in the 1770s, encouraged by the Duke of Atholl.

The gnarled old trunk of this oak measures 5.84 metres (19 feet) in girth and its crown reaches 21.8 metres (71 feet) in height. The bole is heavily decayed and its roots grip tenaciously to the steep riverbank.

The south bank of the River Tay, accessible by public footpath from the bridge at Dunkeld, Perth & Kinross. The site is managed by Forestry Commission Scotland, and public access is available at all times.

The Birks of Aberfeldy

The birches (*Betula spp.*) that clothe the deep glen formed by the Moness Burn, to the south of Aberfeldy, became nationally famous following a visit in 1787 by the nation's bard, Robert Burns. So impressed was he with the natural beauty of the area that he was inspired to write one of his well known works, "The Birks o' Aberfeldie":

> *"Now simmer blinks on flow'ry braes,*
> *And o'er the crystal streamlets plays,*
> *Come let us spend the lightsome days*
> *In the birks of Aberfeldie!"*

As a result, the glen has been maintained as a scenic walk for more than 200 years, and the birch trees have become internationally famous.

Moness Glen, south of Aberfeldy, Perth & Kinross, with access off the A826 road. The glen is owned and maintained by Perth & Kinross Council, and free public access is available at all times.

The Monster Red Cedar

A native of the north west American seaboard, western red cedar
(*Thuya plicata*) was introduced to the United Kingdom in 1853 by
William Lobb (1809 - 1863). A most remarkable specimen stands in a
private estate near Aberfeldy, Perthshire. Many large limbs arise at
ground level from the original tree, and these spread out and layer to
form an ever-increasing circle of new trees. This in turn has created a
huge grove of twisted and bowed trunks that cover a huge area. Many
of the individual trunks are very large, and the volume of timber in this
one breathtaking specimen must be equivalent to the timber content of
a small woodland.

*The private grounds of Findynate
House, on the north bank of the
River Tay, near Aberfeldy, Perth
& Kinross. Access is available
only by permission.*

Diana's Grove

Diana's Grove, in the grounds of Blair Castle, Perthshire, is an outstanding collection of breathtaking conifers that have attained tremendous size. The grove was established between 1872 and 1880 as a tribute to the Roman goddess of hunting. Many trees exceed 45 metres (150 feet) tall, and the grove contains several of the largest trees in the United Kingdom.

The noble fir (*Abies procera*), which is tree number 11 in the grove, is a superb specimen with a clean, straight trunk for the first 10 metres (33 feet). Its overall height is 50 metres (165 feet), and the trunk has a girth of 3.96 metres (13 feet). This handsome species was discovered and introduced by David Douglas in 1830.

> *The grounds of Blair Castle, off the A9 highway about 56 kilometres (35 miles) north of Perth. The castle and grounds are open to the public. Admission charges apply.*

The Cluny Redwood

ince its introduction to Scotland in 1853 by John Matthew of Perthshire, the giant redwood (*Sequoiadendron giganteum*) has become an instantly recognisable feature in the Scottish landscape. Its elegant spire invariably towers above surrounding trees or stands aloof in policies and parkland. The giant redwood grows extremely rapidly in the Scottish climate and relatively young trees have already reached tremendous size, none more so than the vast specimen at Cluny Garden, near Aberfeldy, Perthshire. With a girth of 11.05 metres (36 feet 3 inches), the largest recorded for any tree in Scotland, this mightily impressive "champion" dominates all around it.

Cluny Garden, sign-posted from an unclassified road along the north bank of the River Tay, about 4 kilo-metres (2.5 miles) east of Aberfeldy, Perth & Kinross. Public access is available and admission charges apply.

The churchyard at Fortingall, about 13 kilometres (8 miles) west of Aberfeldy, Perth & Kinross. Free public access is available all year.

The Fortingall Yew

E stimated to be perhaps 5,000 years old, the Fortingall Yew (*Taxus baccata*) stands at the geographical heart of Scotland. It is believed to be the most ancient tree in the United Kingdom, and is probably even the oldest living thing in Europe.

The tree was first described in 1769 by the Hon. Daines Barrington, who measured its circumference at 16 metres (52 feet). [1] By July 1833 Dr Neil found that large amounts had been cut away "by the country people, with the view of forming quechs or drinking cups, and other relics, which visitors were in the habit of purchasing". [2] The trunk then resembled a semi-circular wall, although new spray and a few young branches were growing to a height of up to 9 metres (30 feet).

In 1854, Loudon said, "its age is unknown, but it has long been a mere shell, forming an arch through which funeral processions were accustomed to pass". [3]

Today this venerable tree is still a very impressive sight, and is enclosed by a wall built to create a sanctuary for its undisturbed growth. Its trunk now comprises several separate elements, and without knowing the tree's long history it would be difficult to regard it as a single tree. The circle of white pegs illustrates the former circumference of the once vast trunk.

Wood engraving of the
tree from "Sylva Britannica" by J.G. Strutt (1830).

The Glen Lyon Ash

A private field near Slatich Farm, about 16 kilometres (10 miles) along Glen Lyon from Fortingall, west of Aberfeldy, Perth & Kinross. It stands close to the public road, from where it can easily be viewed.

One of the largest and oldest examples of native ash (*Fraxinus excelsior*) resides in Perthshire's beautiful Glen Lyon. The moss-covered trunk has an exceptional girth measuring 6.4 metres (21 feet), the largest so far recorded for this species in Scotland. Once reaching 30 metres (98 feet) in height, the crown has been heavily cut back to a stump of some 4 metres (13 feet).

The tree appears to have been pollarded at various times throughout its life. This ancient form of tree management involves cutting the top off the tree to stimulate the production of numerous straight shoots. These are harvested periodically to provide a sustainable source of timber and animal fodder. Pollarding is usually carried out 2 to 4 metres (6.5 to 13 feet) above ground level so that the young growth is out of the reach of grazing animals. Although pollarding can look rather severe when newly carried out, it can be an effective method for securing the future of veteran trees. The Glen Lyon ash has certainly benefited, and is putting on vigorous new growth.

It is possible that this veteran may be between 300 and 400 years old. This is exceptional for ash, which is not known as a long-lived species. Under normal circumstances in Scotland, ash trees can be expected to attain a maximum age of 200 to 250 years before decay and decline set in.

Robertson's Oak

In the aftermath of the Jacobite uprising of 1745, supporters of Bonnie Prince Charlie were ruthlessly hunted down as the Government exerted its iron grip over the Scots. While many fled to France to spend time in enforced exile, some elected to remain on their native soil and cleverly evade capture, using all the resourcefulness and ingenuity they could muster. One such individual was George Robertson of Faskally, a well-known supporter of the Stuart kings and loyal follower of the Young Pretender.

While being pursued by a band of Redcoats in 1746 he is said to have taken refuge within the branches of an oak tree. Hiding amidst its verdant foliage, his pursuers passed by unaware of his presence and he subsequently evaded capture, and certain death. A tree known as The Robertson Oak (*Quercus robur*) stands to this day in the Highland Perthshire town of Pitlochry and is reputedly the very tree within which Robertson made good his escape. A small iron plaque set in a concrete plinth was erected by the Clan Donnachaidh Society in 1968 to commemorate the tree's significance in Scottish history.

However, time and people have not been kind to this named tree. It stands unceremoniously next to the town's sewage works, a rather neglected and forlorn specimen in a far from fitting location. Decay has taken hold of the trunk and the crown is showing signs of extensive dieback, with the tree exhibiting a definite stag-headed appearance. It is not particularly large in terms of girth, and it is doubtful whether this particular tree is old enough to have provided shelter for the fugitive Jacobite. The girth of the trunk is 1.3 metres (4 feet 4 inches) and the height 15.6 metres (51 feet) to the tip of the live foliage.

Off the main A9 road which enters Pitlochry, Perth & Kinross, from the south, just north of the petrol filling station on the west side, at the entrance to the sewage works. The tree is hidden behind a conifer hedge.

The Madroña at Castle Menzies

Castle Menzies stands north of the River Tay at the village of Weem, on the B846, 2.4 kilometres (1.5 miles) from Aberfeldy, Perth & Kinross. It is open from 1st April (or Easter) to mid-October, 10.30am - 5pm (Sundays, 2 - 5pm). Admission charges apply.

Madroña (*Arbutus menziesii*), is a native of north west America. It was first discovered and recorded by Archibald Menzies (1754 - 1842) in 1792, in what is now Washington State. Appropriately, it was named after him. Menzies was born near Castle Menzies, near Aberfeldy in Perthshire, and it was here that he first became interested in botany and the natural world. After training in medicine at Edinburgh, he was appointed in 1790 as surgeon/naturalist on board HMS Discovery, under the command of Captain Vancouver. Before setting off, Menzies was charged by Sir Joseph Banks of Kew Gardens to record and collect plants on his travels around the world. In this respect he certainly made his name, with many new discoveries attributed to him. However, it wasn't until 1827 that the species was introduced to the United Kingdom by David Douglas.

The tree at Castle Menzies was planted about 1870 by Sir Robert Menzies (1844 - 1930), thereby commemorating an illustrious member of the clan. [1] It is probably one of the oldest surviving examples of the species in Scotland.

The most striking feature of madroña is the cinnamon-red bark, which peels off in long, curly strips, like the bark of many species of eucalyptus. It is sometimes referred to as the strawberry tree because of its small orange-red fruits, which create a striking contrast with the tree's large, glossy evergreen foliage.

The Kenmore Coast Redwoods

A pair of exceptional coast redwoods (*Sequoia sempervirens*) stand amidst a grove of giant conifers on the northern bank of scenic Loch Tay, near the village of Kenmore. The trees form part of the estate of nearby Taymouth Castle, the ancestral home of the Earls of Breadalbane. The lofty canopies display distinctive feathery foliage, and the single, straight trunks have characteristic thick, spongy bark. This bark acts as a defence mechanism against the forest fires which intermittently sweep through its native habitat.

The Scottish explorer Archibald Menzies was the first European to officially discover the species in 1795, but it was not until 1843 that it eventually reached these shores, via Russia. It is thought that the Kenmore trees are very early introductions, or possibly originals. The trees are flourishing in the Perthshire climate, and are arguably the finest and largest examples of the species in Scotland. In 2005,

the larger of the two trees measured a very respectable 7.9 metres (26 feet) in girth and 42.8 metres (140 feet 5 inches) in height. However, they have a long way to go to catch up with their forebears, which grow in a narrow strip along the fog-shrouded coastal seaboard of north west America: the tallest tree in the world is the recently discovered and appropriately named "Stratosphere Giant", which stands at a staggering 112.5 metres (369 feet). [1]

The trees stand within a grove of giant conifers on the north eastern bank of Loch Tay, at the village of Kenmore, Perth & Kinross. They can be reached on foot from a car park on the west side of the road, just north of the bridge over the river Tay on the A827 (opposite the caravan site). Head west along the public footpath at the side of the loch, past the holiday property complex on the right, for approximately 400 metres (440 yards). The trees stand on the right hand side of the path.

The Stewart Larch

On the road from Pitlochry to Tummel Bridge, Perth & Kinross. The tree is in the grounds of Bonskeid House, and access is available only by prior arrangement.

The fine, open-grown European larch (*Larix decidua*) that stands outside Bonskeid House, near Pitlochry in Perthshire, was planted in 1795. The earliest history regarding the lands of Bonskeid told how Robert the Bruce was a fugitive there after his defeat at the battle of Methven in 1306. The land was then granted to one of the Stewarts of Garth, a great grandson of the noted "Wolf of Badenoch", himself a great-grandson of Robert the Bruce.

Alexander Stewart (1753-1835), descendant of the Stewarts of Garth, was a medical student at Edinburgh University and became a doctor at Dunkeld. From there he used to ride to Bonskeid to look after his property. He was a friend of the Duke of Atholl, who gave him some of the seed of the original larch trees introduced into Scotland (see the Parent Larch page 134), which he planted on the lawn outside the house.

Now more than 200 years old, this beautiful tree is known as the Stewart Larch. It is still going strong and stands tall in this beautiful setting. Originally a private home, the property was for a while a youth hostel, allowing many to view this beautiful tree. However, the tree in now once again in private hands, and although it can be viewed, prior booking is necessary.

The Rannoch Crab

In the first edition of *Heritage Trees of Scotland*, a tree called St Boswell's Apple was included as the largest crab apple (*Malus sylvestris*) in Scotland at 2.41 metres (8 feet) in girth. During the preparation for this edition, Archie Miles and Jon Stokes were exploring along the southern edge of Loch Rannoch, looking for ancient Scots pines, when they discovered this delightful tree, growing close to the road along the southern edge of the loch.

The substantial trunk of this squat tree measures a massive 2.89 metres (9 feet 6 inches) in circumference, showing that ancient trees can be growing in the most unlikely places, and making this newly found tree one of the largest crab apples in Britain.

On the southern shore of Loch Rannoch, Perth & Kinross Take the road from Kinloch Rannoch for 14.5 kilometres (9 miles), and the tree can be found growing beside the road, about 46 metres (50 yards) from the loch's edge.

WESTERN SCOTLAND

Scenically spectacular, the west of Scotland is a great place to live if you're a tree. Gentle, moisture-laden south westerly winds, aided and abetted by the benign Gulf Stream, produce ideal conditions for the famous oakwoods of the Atlantic seaboard: Scotland's own temperate rain forests. These oakwoods are remnants of the original ancient woodland which spread and thrived here after the last Ice Age. A glance at the map, though, will show you how few heritage trees exist here. Exceptional and inspiring enclaves such as Sutherland's Grove, Inverary and Ardkinglas (supporting one of the tallest and possibly the largest conifer in Europe) exist because visionary estate owners, sheltered local conditions and champion-producing growth rates came together in a rare combination.

Farther east lie the scenic splendours of Loch Lomond and the Trossachs, Scotland's first National Park. Intersecting the park is the Highland fault line, a striking divide between lowland and upland Scotland, separating – geographically speaking – very different regions with very different characteristics. A cluster of remarkable trees not far from Loch Lomond creates a centre of interest for seekers of heritage trees, including the Duelling Trees, the Clachan Oak, the Poker Tree and Robert the Bruce's Yew.

Readers might wonder why so few heritage trees feature on Scotland's islands. With a much harsher growing environment – salty, wind-blown and exposed – the scope for growing long-lived trees here is much less than on the mainland. Add to that a lack of landed estates, and it becomes clear why so few examples gain a mention on the roll call of heritage trees. The Arran Whitebeams, however, are a notable exception, although they are comparative dwarfs in the world of heritage trees.

An oak in Loch Lomond.

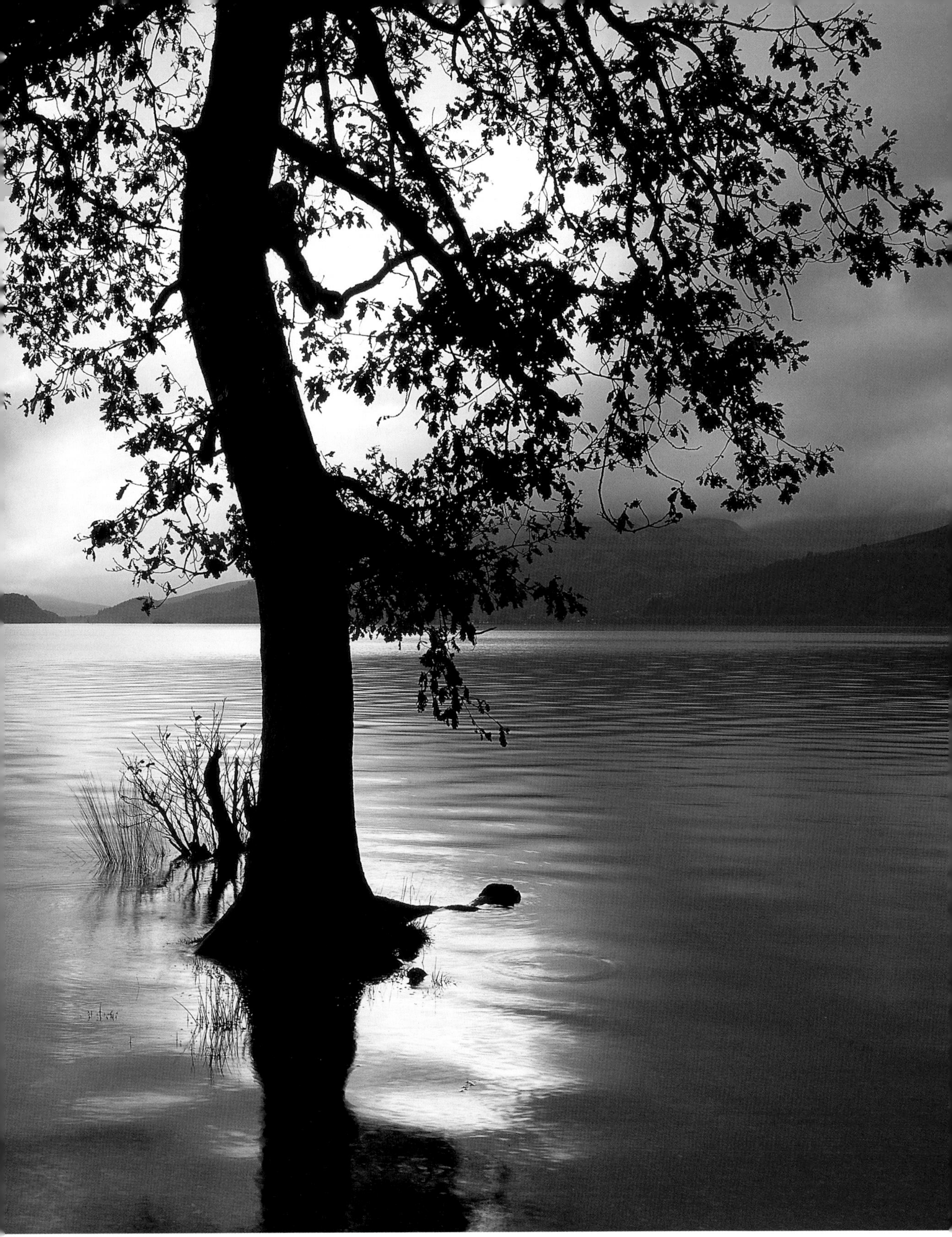

WESTERN SCOTLAND

Inveraray
105/106
107
104
Callander
109 Doune
103 110 102
108 101
Lochgilphead
97 Dunblane
99
Dunoon
98 Stirling
93 100
Rothesay 91 Falkirk
92 Renfrew 86
89 Glasgow
Paisley 90 97 Motherwell
95 88
96 Millport
94

Campbeltown

111

Queen Mary's Tree

This single, open-grown specimen of sweet chestnut (*Castanea sativa*) constitutes one of many parkland trees which form the designed landscape surrounding Cumbernauld House, in North Lanarkshire. Its vast trunk measures 2.18 metres (7 feet 2 inches) in diameter and 6.85 metres (22 feet 6 inches) in girth, and its gnarled and twisted appearance bears testament to a long and hard life. Its canopy is healthy and vigorous and has attained a height of 13.8 metres (45 feet).

Not only is it a fine and ancient example of its species, it also enjoys a royal provenance. It is reputed to have been planted by Mary, Queen of Scots, in 1561 during a visit to Cumbernauld

Castle. The original castle was built in 1371 by the Fleming family, who held tenure for many years. It was a certain Mary Fleming who had the royal connection, being one of the Queen's "Four Marys". These four young ladies were chosen by the Queen's mother, Mary of Guise, to be companions to her daughter; their families were connected with the royal house of Stewart and had close associations with France. Whether by accident or design, all had the first name of Mary. It was Mary Fleming, along with her brother, Lord Fleming, who went with Mary, Queen of Scots into exile in France. The castle no longer exists, and has been replaced by a fine neo-classical mansion, built by William Adam in 1731. The ancient sweet chestnut survives, and commemorates the strong bond between two notable figures in Scotland's history.

Another, less impressive, sweet chestnut lies to the rear of the house and this probably dates from the same period.

Cumbernauld House lies on the north east edge of the town of Cumbernauld, North Lanarkshire. It is best accessed from the north off the A8011 Central Way, where the entrance drive is signposted "Cumbernauld Theatre". Follow straight along the drive to the house, where parking is available. The tree stands 130 metres (142 yards) to the south of the house, in open parkland. Cumbernauld House Park is owned and managed by North Lanarkshire Council, and there is free public access throughout the year.

The Covenanters' Oak

Alone veteran known as the Covenanters' Oak stands just off the main avenue to historic Dalzell House, on the outskirts of Motherwell, North Lanarkshire. It takes its name from the members of the Scottish Presbyterian movement which, in 1638, covenanted to defend their church from the influence of Charles I and his attempt to introduce the English Prayer Book. The Hamilton family, who held Dalzell Estate at the time, were sympathetic to the Covenanters' cause and provided protection to its more troublesome ringleaders. One such notable character was the Reverend John Lauder, who is said to have preached to 400 Covenanters under the boughs of the great oak, which provided a natural gathering point for clandestine religious meetings.

The huge English, or pedunculate, oak (*Quercus robur*) is thought to be an isolated survivor of an extensive deer park and hunting estate planted by King David I in the mid-12th century, which would make it a contemporary of the veterans just across the River Clyde at Cadzow (see page 164). The imposing trunk now measures an impressive 6.69 metres (22 feet) in girth. The fine old oak stands to this day in good health, a living reminder of a tumultuous period in Scotland's religious history.

Next to the main driveway about 400 metres (440 yards) west of Dalzell House in Dalzell Estate, off Dalzell Drive on the southern outskirts of Motherwell, North Lanarkshire. The country park is managed by North Lanarkshire Council, and free public access is available throughout the year.

The Cadzow Oaks

This internationally important group of about 300 sessile oaks (*Quercus petraea*) includes some of the oldest and largest examples of the species in Scotland. They are thought to have been planted by King David I (1124 - 1153) in the mid-12th century, when he used nearby Cadzow Castle as a hunting base. The ancient oaks might indeed be contemporary with King David I, which would rank them among the oldest broadleaved trees in Scotland. This surviving collection of veteran trees now represents a rare example of mediaeval wood pasture. Most of the oaks fall within a Site of Special Scientific Interest because of the unique habitat they provide for rare and endangered insects.

The individual trees are particularly notable for their contorted trunks, which are heavily burred and have great girths. Having grown in an open situation and been subjected to centuries of grazing around them, they have assumed a variety of unusual shapes. Each is a living sculpture with a unique signature of swellings, twists, ridges and cavities. Many trees are noticeably stag-headed, with an array of dead, sun-bleached branches protruding from the live crowns. This is a typical characteristic of veteran trees and part of their natural survival mechanism. As trees age and their trunks start to deteriorate, they conserve resources by dying back and forming new, more compact crowns.

Access to these trees is restricted, but three fine specimens stand in neighbouring Chatelherault Country Park and are accessible to the public. Chatelherault Country Park is on the south east outskirts of Hamilton, South Lanarkshire, and is well signposted off the A72 road. The oaks are signposted from the visitor centre. The Country Park is owned and managed by South Lanarkshire Council, and free public access is available throughout the year.

The Darnley Sycamore

Located incongruously in the heart of urban Glasgow, the once rural setting of this named sycamore (*Acer pseudoplatanus*) has been heavily encroached upon in recent decades by urban sprawl. An isolated survivor of a bygone age, it is now surrounded on all sides by modern housing estates and retail developments.

As its name suggests, it is one of the many trees in Scotland which are claimed to have links with Mary, Queen of Scots. A plaque erected by Glasgow City Council on the iron railings which encloses the tree reads, "...Henry Stewart, Lord Darnley and Mary, Queen of Scots, sat under this great sycamore tree when she nursed him back to health after an illness...". Darnley and Mary married in 1565 and are reputed to have stayed at nearby Crookston Castle.

The sycamore is not especially large in terms of height or girth, with a trunk diameter of 1.3 metres (4 feet 3 inches), a girth of 4.09 metres (13 feet 5 inches), and a height of 18.8 metres (61 feet). It seems unlikely that this particular tree was around at that time to support this romantic tale. For it to have been of a stature large enough to make it attractive for Scotland's queen to sit under would require it to have been around since about 1450, suggesting that it would now be about 550 years old. This is clearly not the case. Something of an arboricultural impostor, it serves as a good example of how trees can assume a false pedigree with the passage of time.

The tree, nevertheless, cuts a fine figure as an open-grown specimen, with long, spreading limbs and an attractive dome-shaped crown typical of the species. The crude removal of lower limbs in the past has resulted in the formation of a number of well developed cavities on the main trunk, from which emerge impressive brackets of the Dryad's saddle fungus (*Polyporous squamossus*), suggesting that the process of internal decay is well advanced. Where stubs have been left, these are now completely calloused over to form outlandish protrusions on the trunk. Numerous nails hammered into the trunk by children to facilitate access into the tree is not doing it any favours, and is part of the price it has to pay for its prominent urban existence.

At the busy junction of the A726 Nitshill Road and Kennishead Road, in the Nitshill district of Glasgow. The tree stands on an area of public open space enclosed within circular iron railings, and is readily accessible at all times of the year.

The Pollok Park Beech

The grossly distorted trunk of this beech (*Fagus sylvatica*) never ceases to amaze visitors. The trunk consists of a swollen and heavily gnarled mass of burrs and branches that appear to have amalgamated through time to form a huge, contorted ball extending from ground level up to 3 metres (9 feet 10 inches). From this massive structure a number of relatively small limbs radiate in all directions to form a low, spreading crown. The trunk is of huge proportions, measuring 7 metres (23 feet) in girth at ground level and expanding to 10 metres (32 feet 10 inches) at its widest point.

Thought to be about 250 years old, this eccentric of the arboricultural world has become a well known focal point in Glasgow's Pollok Park, where it stands atop a small podium in the gardens behind Pollok House. How this prominent tree assumed its outlandish shape is open to conjecture. Perhaps some genetic aberration, coupled with repeated pruning over a long period, might explain its strange form.

The lands of Pollok have been held by the Maxwell family for 700 years. Major plantings by the seventh baronet, Sir John Maxwell (1768 – 1844) and the tenth baronet, Sir John Stirling Maxwell (1866 – 1956), have created a wonderful treescape and lasting legacy for the people of Glasgow.

Pollok Country Park, on the south side of Glasgow. The main access to the park is off Pollokshaws Road. The tree stands prominently in the gardens immediately to the rear of Pollok House. Free public access throughout the year.

169

The Dargarvel Hornbeam

Dargarvel House, about 1.6
kilometres (1 mile) south of
Bishopton, Renfrewshire.
It stands in the grounds of a
large ordnance factory, and
access is strictly controlled.

A remarkable example of hornbeam (*Carpinus betulus*) is the vast, layering specimen that stands near Dargarvel House, at Bishopton, Renfrewshire. It is one of the largest and oldest known in Scotland and is thought to have been planted about the time of major remodelling work to Dargarvel House in 1670.

The low branches of this tree extend over a wide area, taking root and layering as they go. They form a contorted, sprawling mass covering an area of 1320 square metres (one third of an acre). The central hub of this extraordinary tree is a short, squat trunk measuring 4.11 metres (13 feet 6 inches) in girth.

The Craigends Yew

The Craigends yew (*Taxus baccata*) is a sprawling monster of a tree. One of the biggest and oldest of its type in Scotland, the low, layering canopy spreads over the banks of the River Gryffe in Renfrewshire. Large branches descend to ground level, where they take root and proliferate in an impenetrable jungle of tangled growth. The circumference of the crown is quite remarkable, at 100 metres (328 feet), and its huge trunk measures 8.29 metres (27 feet 3 inches) in girth at ground level. The exact age and provenance of the Craigends Yew is unknown, although it is estimated to be between 500 and 700 years old.

The banks of the River Gryffe in Houston, Renfrewshire, next to Yew Tree Gardens. A public foot-path passes close to the tree, which is identified by an interpretation plaque. Free public access is available throughout the year.

John Knox's Yew

The yew tree about to be moved
from its original position in 1900.

Asingle, open-grown yew (*Taxus baccata*) tree stands on the lawn of Finlaystone House, in a commanding, if exposed, position over-looking the Firth of Clyde at Langbank. It is known as John Knox's Yew because legend has it that the austere religious reformer preached under its boughs in the 16th century. A small plaque at the base of tree reads, "Under this tree, in 1556, John Knox is said to have celebrated the first Reformed Communion in the West of Scotland."

The laird of Finlaystone at that time was Alexander Cunningham, the 5th Earl of Glencairn, who was known to be an outspoken supporter of the reformation. Knox appears to have had a habit of preaching al fresco and of using yew trees as a natural pulpit (see the Great Yew of Ormiston, page 80). Yews, with their ancient religious significance and sombre, sheltering canopy, probably provided natural focuses for outdoor services where a congregation could listen to Knox's passionate, if intimidating, sermons.

John Knox's Yew is of no great size for its reputed age. The trunk forks into two stems at ground level with modest girths of 2.28 and 1.8 metres (7 feet 6 inches and 5 feet 11 inches). The neat and compact crown forms a narrow dome, which is tight and springy almost down to ground level, although this has become rather tattered on the west face because of the effects of the prevailing wind. The tree also displays a pronounced lean to the east and is supported with an iron prop which has been placed under the larger stem. Despite its elevated and exposed position close to the coast, it is in good health and condition.

The yew has another story to tell: it is the successful survivor of an ambitious transplanting operation carried out in 1900. The owner of Finlaystone at that time was George Jardine Kidston, a wealthy Clyde shipping magnate. While commissioning extensive refurbishment works and improvements to the house he realised that the dense canopy of Knox's yew was blocking light from the principal rooms. Conscious of the tree's association with Scotland's famous reformer, he was loath to simply fell it. At great expense, he employed an American firm to physically transplant the tree some 30 metres (33 yards) to the south to improve the illumination into the bay windows of the house. This must have been a major pioneering operation in its day. It involved excavating the tree's substantial root-ball and placing a timber sled underneath it. This was then pulled along timber runners along a large trench excavated in the ground to its final resting position. The operation appears to have been a remarkable success. Mature yew trees are notoriously difficult to transplant successfully, and it bears testament to the skill and care which must have been exercised in the process. Knox's yew seems none the worse for its move more than a century ago, and the legend lives on.

The tree stands in the private gardens of Finlaystone House, which is located off the A8 approximately 1.6 kilometres (1 mile) west of the village of Langbank, Renfrewshire. It can be readily viewed from the adjacent Finlaystone Country Park, which is open daily to the public all year from 10.30am to 5pm. Admission charges apply.

The Arran Whitebeams

The Isle of Arran is home to two species of tree which do not occur anywhere else in the world, the Arran whitebeam (*Sorbus arranensis*) and the Arran cut-leaved whitebeam (*Sorbus pseudofennica*). They are also Scotland's rarest native trees, and in global terms are officially classed as dangerously close to extinction by the WWF.

Only a few hundred trees of each species exist, clinging perilously to the steep rocky slopes of two remote glens at the north of the island. The Arran whitebeam was first recorded in 1897, and is thought to have arisen as a natural hybrid between the rock whitebeam (*Sorbus rupicola*) and the ubiquitous rowan (*Sorbus aucuparia*).

Leaves of Sorbus pseudofennica indicate the parents of this hybrid: Sorbus aucuparia and Sorbus arranensis

The other rare hybrid, the Arran cut-leaved whitebeam, was first noted in 1952. This appears to have arisen from the Arran whitebeam back-crossing with the rowan. Both species were more abundant in the past, but have been forced to retreat to their restricted enclaves as the island was progressively improved for agriculture.

Small, windswept and stunted, these uniquely Scottish trees are under constant threat from the strong gales and heavy snow storms common in their montane habitat, because the fragile root systems are easily dislodged from the rocky soil.

Sorbus arranensis tucked well away from the unwanted attentions of the red deer in the depths of the river gorge in Glen Diomhan.

A view of Glen Diomhan reveals the precarious location of these whitebeams.

Glens Catacol and Diomhan, approximately 3.2 kilometres (2 miles) west of Lochranza, Isle of Arran.

175

The Kelburn
Weeping Larch

This outlandish specimen of European larch (*Larix decidua*) in the grounds of Kelburn Castle bears no resemblance to the elegant and graceful form usually associated with the species. Said to have been planted about 1800, the "weeping larch" occupies a prime position in the castle gardens, which overlook the Firth of Clyde, south of Largs, North Ayrshire.

The tree sports a mass of twisting and contorted branches, many of considerable size, which radiate from the short, squat bole and weep to the ground. They proceed to grow haphazardly along the surface for many metres, arching and twisting and throwing up new shoots as they go. Several branches have successfully layered to produce new trees, which in turn are starting to weep and layer, thereby perpetuating the process. Increasing in ever-expanding circles of serpentine branches, this one tree covers almost 0.2 hectares (half an acre).

A fascinating old tree, the Kelburn larch is undoubtedly a mutant monster of the arboricultural world, and probably unique in Britain. However, it is not without considerable character and charm, and is well worth a visit to marvel at its crazy architecture and relentless survival strategy.

Next to the walled garden, or plaisance, of Kelburn Castle, off the A78 road about 1.6 kilometres (1 mile) south of Largs, North Ayrshire. The grounds are managed as a country park and are open to the public for most of the year.

The Kelburn Yews

Within the plaisance, or walled garden, of Kelburn Castle, near Largs, Ayrshire, stands a pair of yews (*Taxus baccata*) reputed to be 1000 years old. The trees, a male and a female, stand side by side 20 metres (64 feet) apart. They are both fine specimens with large boles measuring 5.02 metres (16 feet 6 inches) and 5.18 metres (17 feet) in girth. The branches of one of the trees extend down to ground level, creating a dark inner chamber. Despite the site having been continuously occupied by the Boyle family since 1140, the origin and history of the two yews remain a mystery.

At the entrance to Benmore Botanic Garden, off the A815 road about 11.3 kilometres (7 miles) north of Dunoon, Argyll. The garden is a specialist outpost of the Royal Botanic Garden Edinburgh. Public access is available March to October.

The Benmore
Redwood Avenue

A most impressive example of an avenue of giant redwoods (*Sequoiadendron giganteum*) greets the visitor to Benmore Botanic Garden in Argyll. A single avenue of 48 trees is laid out in a perfectly straight line over a distance of 300 metres (328 yards) from the gatehouse almost to Benmore House itself. It was planted in 1863 by the then owner of Benmore Estate, Piers Patrick.

The avenue is very formal and regular in its layout. Generous spacing between the trees has allowed the unimpeded development of deep, spire-like crowns typical of the species. The largest trees are now more than 50 metres (165 feet) tall and have girths of 6.4 metres (21 feet).

The Duelling Trees

An unusual pair of old sweet chestnuts (*Castanea sativa*), known as the Duelling Trees, remain at Ballencleroch Castle, nestling at the foot of Campsie Glen in East Dunbartonshire. Their name derives from their use as markers in duels. One tree collapsed many years ago and its fallen hulk lies on the ground, but its duelling partner still enjoys good health.

Built about 1423, Ballencleroch Castle came into the hands of James and Mary McFarlan in 1664, and it was about this time that tragedy befell the family. Their son, Hugh, was involved in a duel with a member of the Stirling family at the pair of old chestnut trees. The young Stirling was killed, and Hugh McFarlan had to leave the country hastily for fear of reprisals. Legend has it that the ghost of young Stirling was seen wandering around the chestnut trees for many years.

On joining the army and working abroad, Hugh McFarlan's fortune changed for the better and he eventually returned and settled at Ballencleroch. He is said to have brought back many trees from his foreign travels and planted them in the castle grounds. This pair of ancient sweet chestnuts which still adorn the grounds serves as a grim reminder of tragic events.

The grounds of Ballencleroch Castle, in the hamlet of Clachan of Campsie, off the A891 road about 1.6 kilometres (1 mile) west of Lennoxtown, East Dunbartonshire. The castle is now run by the Schoenstatt Sisters of Mary as a convent and religious retreat. Access is available only with permission.

The Clachan Oak

The ancient sessile oak (*Quercus petraea*) which stands in Balfron, Stirlingshire is clearly a very old tree of some significance, and forms an interesting focal point. It once occupied the central green of an ancient hamlet known as The Clachan, which was ultimately to grow into the village of Balfron.

The tree was recorded in 1867 as being in a "flourishing condition", with a girth of 4.8 metres (15 feet 9 inches) at 1.8 metres (6 feet) above the ground. At that time it was thought to be 334 years old and to have been struck by lightning 40 years before. [1] The short trunk, which is completely hollow, now measures 4.9 metres (16 feet) in girth.

An Edwardian postcard of the tree.

The most notable features of the tree are the three iron hoops which encircle its trunk. Nowadays they play a useful role in holding the hollow shell together, but originally they had a darker function.

Until the end of the 18th century it was common practice to chain petty criminals to the oak tree, where they were subjected to merciless public ridicule. An iron collar was attached around the neck of the unfortunate victims and connected by a length of chain to the iron hoop encircling the trunk of the oak. This form of ritual humiliation was known as "the jougs", and must have been a most unpleasant form of punishment.

A small area of public open space next to the Church of Scotland and the A875 road in Balfron, in Stirling Council area.

182

The King Tree

This sweet chestnut (*Castanea sativa*) is a well known resident of a 1950s housing estate, and shows that heritage trees can turn up in the most unlikely places. Known locally as the King Tree, it is probably more than 400 years old, and once adorned the grounds of 16th century Herbertshire Castle.

The castle grounds were known to be extremely picturesque, with verdant meadows containing many trees. These beautiful grounds were originally used as a royal hunting station, and it is perhaps this association which is remembered in the tree's name.

Although the castle has long since been demolished, the tree survives as a living relic of a bygone era. The lone chestnut, affectionately referred to by its regal title, has become something of a local landmark within its new suburban surroundings.

Its heavily gnarled trunk is huge, with a girth of 8.3 metres (27 feet 3 inches), one of the largest of its species recorded in Scotland. Despite poor treatment in the past, the gaunt, battered crown of the King Tree is still very much alive, its sparse framework of branches producing a fresh flush of foliage each spring.

An area of council-owned public open space at Chestnut Crescent, Dunipace, in the Falkirk Council area.

The Great Yew at Broich

One of Scotland's few layering yews (*Taxus baccata*) stands in the private grounds of Broich House, near Kippen, Stirlingshire. Its single trunk, which measures an impressive 3.86 metres (12 feet 8 inches) in girth, supports an extensive, spreading canopy. The lower branches weep to the ground where they take root, continuing their outward progress in a maze of zig-zag growth. This single tree covers a vast area of ground as a result of this unusual growth habit, and its ever-expanding canopy occupies a circumference of 120 metres (394 feet). The dark and secluded inner chamber formed by the surrounding skirt of layered foliage has a unique atmosphere and, at about eight metres (26 feet) in diameter, could readily accommodate between 20 and 30 people at one time. In good health and condition, the yew is thought to be between 600 and 1000 years old.

Little is known of the yew's origin. It has been suggested that it was planted by monks from the nearby island priory of Inchmahome, on the Lake of Mentieth (see Inchmahome Veterans, page 188), who were in possession of the property in the 12th century. [1] Old buildings taken down near the site in the latter part of the 19th century apparently dated from the 11th century, which adds some credence to this claim. [2]

Private gardens next to Broich House (formerly known as Arngomery), off the B8037 road on the western edge of Kippen, about 19 kilometres (12 miles) west of Stirling. Access is available only with permission.

Inchmahome Veterans

The 13th century priory of Inchmahome, once home to a small community of Augustinian canons, nestles on a small, low-lying island in the middle of the Lake of Mentieth in Stirlingshire. Of the many fine trees on the island, the three veteran sweet chestnuts (*Castanea sativa*) steal the show in terms of antiquity and character. These heavily gnarled individuals are probably more than 400 years old. Although extensively decayed and hollow, they are still very much alive, and are the island's oldest living residents. The girth of their gnarled trunks ranges from 4.4 metres (14 feet 4 inches) to 6 metres (19 feet 8 inches). The largest of the three is known as the Antlered Chestnut because its stag-headed branches resemble the antlers of a deer. [1]

The trees might well have been around when Mary, Queen of Scots paid a visit to the island in 1547. Accompanied by her mother, Mary of Guise, the four-year-old infant queen sought refuge at the priory for three weeks following the English victory at the Battle of Pinkie. A poem penned by the Reverend W M Stirling in 1815 recalls the royal visit:

> " Those giant boughs that wave around
>   My aged hoary head,
>   Were then the tenants of the ground
>   Where walked the royal maid."

Alongside one of the walks radiating from Inchmahome Priory on an island in the Lake of Mentieth, in the Stirling Council area. The priory is in the care of Historic Scotland and public access is available via a small passenger ferry most of the year, except the winter months.

An Edwardian
postcard shows
the poker hanging
from a different
part of the tree.

OAK TREE & BAILIE NICOL JARVIE'S POKER, ABERFOYLE.

The Poker Tree

The Poker Tree is the unusual name given to a gnarled old oak in Aberfoyle, Stirlingshire. An unexceptional specimen, it is the amusing tale associated with it that marks it out as a tree of significance.

Baillie Nicol Jarvie, a colourful Glasgow magistrate and cousin of the infamous outlaw, Rob Roy MacGregor (1671 - 1734), was travelling on business in the wild Highlands. He stopped at an inn in the Clachan of Aberfoyle where, unfortunately, a truculent Highlander took exception to his presence and, drawing his sword, challenged him to a fight. The Baillie, unused to such violent encounters, tried to draw his sword but found it rusted to his scabbard through lack of use. As the fierce Highlander advanced upon him, the desperate Baillie grabbed a poker from the fire and brandished its red hot tip at his assailant. The poker set fire to the Highlander's plaid and sent him fleeing. The browbeaten Highlander later returned to concede defeat and congratulate Baillie on his guile and mettle in battle.

In memory of the Baillie's exploits, the iron poker was later hung from the branches of the old oak tree which stood outside the inn, and became a tourist attraction. Some years ago the poker was removed for safe-keeping. It was then thought to have been lost, but subsequently reappeared.

Enclosed by low, white railings on the north side of the B829 road, at its junction with Manse Road, Aberfoyle, in the Stirling Council area. The tree can be readily viewed from the road.

Robert The Bruce's Yew

On private land near Tarbet, Argyll & Bute.

Perched on a rocky outcrop on the western shore of Loch Lomond is an ancient yew (*Taxus baccata*) associated with King Robert the Bruce. Legend has it that The Bruce took shelter from pursuing enemies under the evergreen canopy, entertaining his troops with tales of valour. Bruce and 200 of his followers welcomed the rest, having spent a whole night and day ferrying themselves across the loch in a single leaky rowing boat which could only hold three men at a time. [1]

A 1920s postcard shows the tree with Loch Lomond in the background.

J C Loudon (1783 - 1843), the influential Scottish writer who chronicled changes in garden design in the early part of the 19th century, paid a visit to The Bruce's yew on his travels. In 1837 he recorded the girth of the trunk at ground level to be 4 metres (13 feet) and the height at 12 metres (39 feet). By 1998 the girth had increased to 6.1 metres (20 feet) and the height reduced to 5.5 metres (18 feet) as a result of heavy pruning in the interim. This suggests an annual ring width of two millimetres, a reasonable rate of increment for a slow-growing species in such a harsh environment. Now past its prime, this old campaigner must be a mere shadow of its former self, yet new sprouts of fresh growth bode well for its future.

The Mightiest Conifer in Europe

The silver fir (*Abies alba*) is a native of central Europe, the Alps and the Pyrenees. The species was introduced into the United Kingdom about the beginning of the 17th century, and the earliest trees recorded are two mentioned by Evelyn as "being planted by Serjeant Newdigate in Harefield Park in 1603". [1] Although mountains are its natural environment, the species thrives throughout the UK.

This specimen is thought to be more than 250 years old, and even in 1881 it was recorded as a huge tree. Mr Wilkie, the estate forester, calculated that it contained 56 tonnes (57 tons) of timber and said that "no true conception of this noble tree can be formed from reading a description of it". [2] About 1910, after a visit by Charles Sargent, once dubbed "the greatest living authority on trees", Niall Diarmid Campbell (10th Duke of Argyll) wrote to the daughter of the owner of Ardkinglas saying, "It is undeniably the mightiest conifer, if not the biggest bole, of any kind in Europe." [3] Indeed, with a girth of 9.4 metres (31 feet), this colossal silver fir tends to stop people in their tracks.

In 1906 the eminent botanist H J Elwes said that he had "never seen anything surpassing it in bulk, even in the virgin forests of Bosnia". [3] This magnificent silver fir is still thriving and will probably continue growing for many years to come.

In 2005 Dr Robert van Pelt of Washington State University measured the timber volume of the tree to be a staggering 140 cubic metres, confirming it as one of the largest trees by volume in Europe.

Ardkinglas Woodland Garden at Cairndow, Argyll & Bute, off the A83 Loch Lomond to Inveraray road, on the eastern shores of Loch Fyne. The garden is open all year during daylight hours. Admission charges apply.

The Ardkinglas Grand Fir

This majestic grand fir (*Abies grandis*) dominates Ardkinglas Woodland Garden, overlooking the shores of Loch Fyne. A native of the Pacific slopes of western North America, the species was discovered in 1825 by the Scots explorer and botanist David Douglas, who introduced it to the United Kingdom in 1831. This Ardkinglas specimen was planted in 1875, when an outstanding collection of conifers was established by the Callander family, then owners of the Argyllshire estate.

Until 1990 the tree enjoyed the distinction of being the tallest in the United Kingdom. However, at a height of 61 metres (200 feet), when measured in 2002, it now lies third, overtaken by the Douglas fir at Reelig Glen (see Dughall Mor, page 230), at 64 metres (210 feet) tall, when measured in 2005. [1]

It did not take long for the Ardkinglas tree to establish its credentials as a record breaker. By 1931, at a mere 56 years old, it was already 30 metres (98 feet) tall and had a girth of 3.36 metres (11 feet). With no let-up in its growth rate, it took only another 53 years to surpass the 60 metre (197 feet) mark, the first tree known to have done so in the UK. The tree's perfectly clean, "gun-barrel" trunk now measures 6.22 metres (20 feet 5 inches) in girth.

Ardkinglas Woodland Garden at Cairndow, Argyll & Bute, off the A83 Loch Lomond to Inveraray road on the eastern shores of Loch Fyne. The garden is open all year during daylight hours. Admission charges apply.

Inveraray Castle Lime Avenue

Perhaps the oldest lime (*Tilia × europaea*) avenue in Scotland, according to estate records, is that at Inveraray Castle, ancestral home of the Dukes of Argyll. Thought to have been planted about 1650, several of the original trees survive to this day. The avenue has become rather fragmented over the years as trees have been lost and the resulting gaps filled by others. However, the overall impact of this formal style of planting still survives, forming an impressive feature within the extensive grounds of the castle. The original trees have huge girths and are densely shrouded in a forest of basal suckers, which make accurate measurement impossible. They are in remarkably good health, despite the length of time they have had to withstand the harsh Argyll climate.

Lime became widely planted in Scotland from the early 18th century, its reliability of establishment and regularity of growth making it particularly suitable for avenue planting. Avenues of lime quickly became de rigueur for the discerning landowner, especially during the Victorian era, and most country houses boast such a feature today. It is in this formal layout that most limes are encountered, where they form some of the most striking features in designed landscapes.

Along an avenue running north west of Inveraray Castle, off the A83 road on the north shore of Loch Fyne, at Inveraray, Argyll & Bute. Public access is available.

The Balmaha Oak

This well known veteran stands in Balmaha Boatyard, on the southern shores of Loch Lomond. It is a remarkable survivor from a bygone age when the oak coppice industry was an important form of forest management in the area. The tree clearly displays the legacy of coppicing, with three huge trunks arising at ground level. These in turn form a single, spreading canopy. The large trunks are heavily burred and gnarled, and present an intriguing sight. Their collective volume is impressive, and the girth measured at ground level is an amazing 9.73 metres (31 feet).

The Bicycle Tree

Nestled close to the heart of Loch Lomond & the Trossachs National Park lies the small village of Brig o' Turk. Famous for its famous visitors: Queen Victoria, Wordsworth, Millais and Ruskin, it's also well known as the gateway to Glen Finglas, one of Scotland's largest new native woodland plantings. However, not many people know the village as home to one of Scotland's arboricultural curiosities – the Bicycle Tree (also know as the "Metal-Eating Tree" or the "Iron Tree").

This century-old sycamore (*Acer pseudoplatanus*) has almost swallowed up what was once an anchor, and a bicycle. It occupies a spot close to the old smiddy (smithy), and local folklore has it that the village blacksmith was in the habit of propping up or hanging various articles, which were then forgotten about and gradually absorbed by the "ironivorous" tree. There is a story about a villager conscripted to the Great War who left his bicycle over a branch. Perhaps he never returned, or perhaps on his return he found that the tree had claimed the bicycle as its own. Today all that remains sticking out of the trunk is the handlebars: an unusual testimony to nature's efforts overcoming Man's.

Its metal diet seems to have done the tree no harm, and it has certainly outlived the blacksmith, who is buried close by in the little graveyard up the lane. The eponymous local newspaper, "The Bicycle Tree", provides another lasting reminder of this strange, metal-devouring sycamore.

On the west side of the Glen Finglas road about 1 kilometre (half a mile) north of Brig o' Turk. The village is 15 kilometres (9 miles) west of Callander, in the Stirling Council area, on the A821.

The Fairy Tree

A Scots pine (*Pinus sylvestris*) stands sentinel on the summit of Doon Hill, on the outskirts of Aberfoyle. Known as the Fairy Tree, it is steeped in mystery and intrigue.

An unremarkable tree of no great age or extraordinary character, it has an interesting story to tell. This centres around the Reverend Robert Kirk, a learned and respected minister in the Parish of Aberfoyle in the latter half of the 17th century. After a distinguished, if somewhat conventional, career, his mind started to turn to subjects supernatural. This was to culminate in 1691 with the publication of an extraordinary book entitled "The Secret Commonwealth of Elves, Fauns and Fairies", in which he describes in intimate detail his encounters and conversations with the fairy people on Doon Hill. For the first time, this was to graphically divulge the secrets of the Scottish supernatural underworld to the mortal population, a rash and ill-considered act which was ultimately to lead to the minister's undoing.

In 1692, aged 48 years, Robert Kirk fell down in a fit whilst walking on Doon Hill, and mysteriously passed away. After returning briefly to haunt his relatives, his ghost was never seen again. It is said that, as retribution for divulging the secrets of the fairy kingdom, he was spirited away to fairyland, where he remains trapped to this day. Legend has it that the old pine tree on Doon Hill contains the spirit of the unfortunate minister, confined for eternity inside an arboreal prison.

Doon Hill's association with spirits and fairies lives on to this day. The pine tree provides the focus for this fascination, and the well-worn path to the top of the hill bears testament to its many visitors. A "cloutie well" has sprung up around the tree, with nearby young oaks festooned with dangling, multi-coloured strips of material, each with a "wish" scrawled on it. Coins have also been pressed deep into the rugged bark of the trunk as a lucky offering to the hill's unearthly inhabitants.

Doon Hill lies 1.6 kilometres (1mile) to the south of Aberfoyle, in the Stirling Council area. A well-marked footpath to the summit is sign-posted from Manse Road, which runs south from the western end of the town's main street.

Rannoch Rowan

An expansive view across Rannoch Moor shows the true isolation of this tree.

Probably the loneliest tree in Britain is a rowan (*Sorbus aucuparia*) which stands in splendid isolation in the desolate wilderness of Rannoch Moor. It perches on top of a giant boulder, its windswept crown bearing testament to the extreme exposure with which it has to contend. Remarkably, the tree has managed to maintain a hold in the crevices of its lichen-encrusted pedestal, its roots somehow seeking sustenance from a deep fissure in the rock. This lonely rowan is now a well-known landmark on the busy A82 road.

The secret of the tree's survival is its elevated position, which keeps it out of reach of the relentless grazing by sheep and deer. Rowan, a species native to Scotland, is an opportunist of the tree world, and this particular tree has carved out its own niche in a harsh environment.

Rannoch Moor was not always so bleak and treeless. Between 5000 and 2500 years ago, Scotland's climate was drier and more continental, causing the bogs to dry out briefly. A vast forest of birch and pine colonised the moor, only to disappear as the climate gradually changed again. All that now remains are countless stumps entombed in a peaty grave, and a small remnant of native pinewood known as the Black Wood of Rannoch.

Beside the A82 trunk road between Glen Coe and Bridge of Orchy, near the boundary between Highland and Perth & Kinross. Public access is available.

NORTHERN SCOTLAND

"Land of the Mountain and the Flood", the Highlands bring to mind scenes worthy of Landseer – purple heather, roaring stags and misty rugged mountains. Much fought over, the Highlands' bloody reminders of clan fueds and battles with the English are kept alive in folklore and song. Historically, the Highland clearances – where people were replaced by sheep – suggest a remote landscape devoid of all but the occasional tree. But although this is true for some of northern Scotland's great mountain ranges such as the Cairngorms and the Monadhliaths, the glens are often clothed with the restored remnants of once-extensive native woodlands and the introductions of more modern productive forests. Although this emptiness runs counter to many people's ideas about heritage trees, even remote moorlands such as Rannoch can support 'miracle trees' such as the Rannoch Rowan, where the seedlings remain out of reach of hungry deer and sheep.

Off the exposed peatlands, where more fertile conditions exist, trees enjoy a better growing environment. In fact the tallest tree so far recorded in the UK is found at Dughall Mor near Inverness. Also close to Inverness – clustered around the Black Isle – are a clutch of worthy heritage trees such as Duncan Forbes Oak, the Fairburn Sitka, the Darnaway Oak and the Castle Leod Redwood.

Like the western isles, the northern isles are largely treeless – mainly as a result of exposure to salt-laden winds. But no description of Highland Heritage trees would be complete without a mention of Scotland's remotest heritage tree, the Big Tree of Orkney, a fitting reminder that even in places seemingly inhospitable for tree growth, the fortitude and perseverance of such trees can endure – against all the odds.

Part of the old Caledonian pine forest around Loch Affric.

NORTHERN
SCOTLAND

Thurso

Tongue

Wick

Stornoway

Lochinver

Lairg

Ullapool

Dornoch

Gairloch

△133

△132

Lossiemouth

Cullen   Banff

Uig

△130/31

Alness

Elgin

Dingwall

Cromarty

△121

Keith

Portree

Fortrose

Nairn

Peterhead

△128   △129

△126

△122

△120

Kyle Of Lochalsh

△124

△125

Inverness

Ellon

Grantown-on-Spey

△118

△119

Inverurie

△123

Aviemore

Fort Augustus

Kingussie

Aberdeen

Mallaig

Ballater

△116

Banchory

△115

Stonehaven

△117

Fort William

△113

Tobermory

△112

△114

The Drumtochty Sitka

Archibald Menzies
(1754 – 1842)

This giant Sitka spruce (*Picea sitchensis*) grows in Drumtochty Glen, near Fettercairn, Aberdeenshire. One of the largest-girthed examples so far recorded for this species in Scotland, it measures an impressive 6.78 metres (22 feet 3 inches) in girth. Its height is equally remarkable, at 50 metres (164 feet). It has a superb shape and is a fine example of a species that has radically changed the face of Scottish forestry.

Sitka spruce, a native of the Pacific north west of North America, owes its now ubiquitous presence in the United Kingdom to a pair of pioneering Scots. Discovered by Archibald Menzies in 1792, it was introduced to these shores by the prolific plant collector David Douglas in 1832. However, it was not until the formation of the Forestry Commission in 1919 that the species received any particular attention. It soon became apparent to those charged with regenerating the UK's much depleted woodland resource that Sitka was the new "wonder tree", thriving in the mild, wet Scottish climate and with a capacity to produce high yields on poor sites. These features rapidly endeared it to a fast-developing forestry industry, and today Sitka continues to play a vital role in the nation's timber supply.

Alongside a Forestry Commission Scotland car park on an unclassified road that runs east from the B974 road from a junction about 4.8 kilometres (3 miles) north of Fettercairn, Aberdeenshire, at the Clatterin' Brig Restaurant. An interpretation board and free public access are available throughout year.

The Seven Men of Moidart

The Seven Men of Moidart are a line of beech trees (*Fagus sylvatica*) that commemorate the seven companions who landed with Bonnie Prince Charlie in 1745, when he raised the standard at nearby Glenfinnan. Thought to have been planted early in the 19th century, only five of the original seven trees remain as living monuments to those involved in this pivotal event in Scotland's past. A severe storm in 1988 caused extensive damage to the trees, which occupy a picturesque but highly exposed Highland setting on the northern shore of Loch Moidart.

The surviving "five men" are of great size, with huge and heavily buttressed trunks ranging in girth from 4.3 metres (14 feet) to 5.18 metres (17 feet). However, they are in poor condition and the trunks are badly decayed. These fine old veterans are living on borrowed time: the next big storm that sweeps up the glen is likely to result in more casualties. Nevertheless, the surviving "companions" are fine old trees which commemorate an important historical occasion.

Location: About 600 metres (660 yards) south of the A861 in a private field near Kinlochmoidart, Highland. Roadside parking and an interpretation cairn are available, but access to the trees is restricted.

Sutherland's Grove

A fine stand of about 100 specimen Douglas fir (*Pseudotsuga menziesii*) and Sitka spruce (*Picea sitchensis*) occupy a sheltered hillside known as Sutherland's Grove overlooking Loch Creran at Barcaldine Forest near Oban, Argyll. The grove's origins date back to 1870, when the Camerons of Midlothian acquired the estate from the Campbells. It is almost certain that the planting was not at the time commemorative, but rather one of the "improvement" plantings then popular amongst estate owners.

Today the trees stand an average 46 metres (150 feet) tall, with the tallest recorded at more than 50 metres (164 feet). Their straight, clean trunks are of equally impressive size, measuring up to 4.96 metres (16 feet 3 inches) in girth. The conifers extend up the Abhainn Teithil burn (in Glen Dubh gorge) along an established and waymarked Forestry Commission trail. Some of the largest and most impressive trees stand on this atmospheric section of the walk.

On a granite boulder in the heart of the grove is an inscription in memory of Sir John Donald Sutherland, Forestry Commissioner for Scotland between 1934 and 1942. His ashes are scattered among the giant firs, in the grove that bears his name.

Sutherland's Grove, sign-posted off the A828 about 19 kilometres (12 miles) north of Oban, Argyll & Bute. The site is managed by Forestry Commission Scotland, and parking, an interpretive panel and free public access are available all year.

The Twin Trees of Finzean

Growing in a small stand of pine on the Finzean Estate in Aberdeenshire, these two remarkable Scots pine trees (*Pinus sylvestris*) have formed a most unusual natural arch. Many years ago, a branch from one of the trees naturally grafted itself on to its neighbour, forever joining the two together. The Twin Trees, as they have become known, are an arboricultural curiosity, even featuring in old postcards of the area. Now about 100 years old, the pair of pines make a distinctive local landmark.

Next to the B976 road on the eastern outskirts of the hamlet of Finzean, Aberdeenshire. The trees are readily visible from the public road.

Queen of the Firs

One of Scotland's finest and most impressive Scots pine trees (*Pinus sylvestris*) stands at Ballogie Estate, near Aboyne, Aberdeenshire. It is known affectionately as the Queen of the Firs, because Scots pine used to be known as Scots fir. It is easy to see why this specimen has assumed its regal title, because it is of exceptionally large size for the species, with a girth of 4.71 metres (15 feet 6 inches) and a towering height of 37 metres (121 feet). The single, straight trunk is clean and branch-free for most of its length, with a beautiful tracery of bark markings. It is recorded as having been planted in 1792, and has been frequently measured over the past 100 years.

On the edge of woodland lining the private drive to Ballogie House, off the B976 road about 5.6 kilometres (3.5 miles) south east of Aboyne, Aberdeenshire. Access is available only with permission.

A mighty specimen tree stands proudly in
Ballochbuie Forest (above), whilst some of the
oldest trees may well be typified by gnarled and
stunted forms, which have been of little use to
the forester (opposite).

The estate is reached from the A93
highway. Turn off at Crathie village,
Aberdeenshire, and follow the signs
for Balmoral. Old trees can be found
around the Glenbeg burn area of
Ballochbuie, 6.5 kilometres (4 miles)
west of Balmoral Castle.

The Oldest Scots Pine?

No tree symbolises Scotland, and particularly the Highlands, more than the Scots pine, and there is no doubt that if the identity of the oldest living Scots pine in Scotland were conclusively known, it would qualify for a page in this book. Sadly, no one knows for sure where Scotland's oldest Scots pine is. The oldest one ever scientifically dated stands in Glen Loyne, Inverness-shire, and was estimated to be about 550 years old in the late 1990s by scientists from the Forestry Commission's Forest Research agency. It was one of a group of ancient pines whose average age was put at about 440 years.

Unfortunately the Glen Loyne "granny" pine is inaccessible to the public, but tree enthusiasts who want to enjoy the experience of being among very old Scots pine should head for Ballochbuie Forest, on the Queen's Balmoral Estate.

The exact location of the oldest Scots pine (*Pinus sylvestris*) in Scotland is open to speculation. The original native forest was severely diminished over centuries, through the depredations of fire, grazing, encroachment and logging. Despite this, there still remain several areas of native Caledonian pinewood which date back to the original "wildwood" and, encouragingly, many of these are now being actively extended. Several such remnants exist within Ballochbuie Forest, part of Balmoral Estate in upper Deeside, Aberdeenshire.

One of the earliest recorded acts of native woodland conservation occurred in 1878, when Queen Victoria intervened in a major timber sale. She purchased Ballochbuie with the expressed intention of preventing the old Caledonian pines being sold to an Aberdeen timber merchant. This pinewood has since been preserved by successive generations of the Royal Family, and now contains one of the largest remnants of Caledonian forest remaining in Scotland today.

It's also one of the oldest: recent studies by Macaulay Institute of Aberdeen have dated Ballochbuie Scots pine to more than 400 years old. Precisely where the oldest specimen exists is still to be determined, but the visitor to Balmoral will gain a sense of the elderly – and of renewal through regeneration – by absorbing the spirit of these iconic heritage trees of Scotland.

The Leith Hall Dule Tree

Some of Scotland's trees have a dark and grim past. One of the best known "dule" trees, or hanging trees, stands in the grounds of Leith Hall, near Huntly, Aberdeenshire. This tree, a sycamore (*Acer pseudoplatanus*), was used as a natural gibbet, its strong timber being ideal for the purpose.

Leith Hall dates from about 1650, and the tree might have been planted shortly after this. A rather gaunt and heavily branched specimen, the trunk measures 3.64 metres (12 feet) in girth. There are few surviving dule trees left in Scotland, so this one provides a poignant reminder of harsher times (see also Blairquhan Dool Tree, page 34 and The Gallows Tree, page 126).

The grounds of Leith Hall, about 5.6 kilometres (3.5 miles) north east of Rhynie, Aberdeenshire, on minor roads north of the B9002. Leith Hall is owned by the National Trust for Scotland, and the gardens and grounds are open all year.

The Queen's Tree

On the lawns to the front of Pitcaple Castle, in the heart of rural Aberdeenshire, stands a wych elm (*Ulmus glabra*) with an interesting royal provenance. A plaque at the base of the trunk reads:

> "This tree was planted in place of a thorn tree under which Mary, Queen of Scots, is reported to have danced when she visited Pitcaple in 1562. It was still alive and green in 1850, but its withered stump fell down a few years later."

Unlike its predecessor, the elm enjoys good health, despite losing its top in a storm, and continues to keep the story alive. Its trunk now measures 3.76 metres (12 feet 4 inches) in girth.

Pitcaple Castle is approximately 6.4 kilometres (4 miles) north west of Inverurie, Aberdeenshire, on minor roads just north of the A96 highway. It is in private ownership and access is possible only with permission.

Darnaway's Champion Oak

The largest-girthed broadleaved tree in Scotland is a sessile oak (*Quercus petraea*) that stands in a narrow strip of ancient woodland at the Meads of St John, on Morayshire's Darnaway Estate. Its trunk measures an incredible 9.73 metres (31 feet) in girth. The oak is also very old, recent research using trunk diameter and core samples estimating it to be about 730 years old. [1]

This mighty "champion" is one of several ancient oaks standing on the banks of the River Findhorn. These are thought to be survivors of the vast Royal Forest of Tarnaway, which once clothed the fertile lowlands of Morayshire in medieval times. Much of the forest was felled in the Middle Ages to provide timber for ships, castles and houses, although it was still renowned for its oak at the end of the 19th century. Proceedings of the Royal Scottish Arboricultural Society noted in 1881:

"The oak forest of Darnaway is acknowledged to be the finest in Scotland, and there are few which can compare with it anywhere in the British Isles. For a century the oak produce from this forest, which is over 3000 acres in extent, has attracted attention from all over the north of Scotland…" [2]

Between 1830 and 1840, annual sales of oak timber and bark ranged from £4000 to £5000, a princely sum for the time. Indeed, the revenue of the forest per acre was double that of the finest arable land in the county. [1]

> *In a small area of woodland fringing the west bank of the River Findhorn at the Meads of St John on the Darnaway estate, near Forres, Moray. Access is available only by permission.*

Gordon Castle Ash

The mighty ash (*Fraxinus excelsior*) which stands on the lawns to the front of Gordon Castle, in the Morayshire town of Fochabers, presents an imposing figure. The trunk is of exceptional girth for this species, measuring a staggering 7.79 metres (25 feet 7 inches) in girth at 1m (3 feet 3 inches) above ground level. Above this, the girth becomes grossly exaggerated because of large swellings and limb bases, attaining 8.74 metres (28 feet 8 inches) at 1.5 metres (4 feet 11 inches) above ground. The huge, stately canopy is equally impressive, with the massive limbs which form the framework of the crown reaching 28.5 metres (93 feet 6 inches) in height. The tree appears to have been pollarded (see Glen Lyon Ash, page 150) many years ago, and displays a typically low-branching and multi-stemmed crown form. As is typical with most old ash trees, the trunk is heavily decayed and largely hollow. It is a remarkable testament to the strength of its timber that the thin outer shell of sound wood is capable of supporting such a capacious canopy.

Ash as a species is relatively short-lived, with few trees exceeding 200 years before old age and decay set in. The Gordon Castle tree is clearly something of an exception, and is of considerable antiquity. The site has been a stronghold of the Gordon Clan since the 15th century, with the original castle of 1470 being replaced by the 4th Duke of Gordon in 1769. It is likely the tree dates from around this time.

The entrance to Gordon Castle is located at the west end of the town of Fochabers, approximately 9 miles east of Elgin, Moray. The impressive entrance gates lie to the north of the A98 road at the war memorial, just at the entrance to the west end of the main street. The ash tree stands on the lawns to the north of the castle. Access available with permission.

The Kilravock Castle Layering Beech

eeches (*Fagus sylvatica*) with a tendency to layer are extremely rare in Scotland. Of the very few specimens known to exist, the finest and largest is that which graces the grounds of Kilravock Castle, Inverness-shire. The huge trunk measures 4.9 metres (16 feet) in girth at 1 metre (3.3 feet) above ground level, and it is surrounded by low, snaking limbs which bend to the ground and take root. Some of the layered stems are of considerable size and now form small trees in their own right. The tree has been repeatedly pollarded in the past, and the typically dense, multi-stemmed crown is still in good condition. Thought to have been planted in the latter half of the 17th century, it is of considerable age for a species not known for longevity.

The tree is also known as the Kissing Beech, after a member of an early owner's family and a housemaid were witnessed in an illicit embrace under its spreading limbs. The extensive carving of lovers' names on the bark suggests that many others have used this tree as a rendezvous. The attraction of lovers to beech trees has led to many other old beeches being known as "trysting trees" because "of their smooth grey bark in which letters of devotion, hearts and arrows of desire have long been scribed". [1]

Kilravock Castle (pronounced Kilrawck), built in 1460, has seen many famous visitors over the centuries, including Mary, Queen of Scots in 1562 and Robert Burns in 1787. Bonnie Prince Charlie is reputed to have been entertained within its thick walls the day before the Battle of Culloden in 1746.

On a low bank alongside the driveway to Kilravock Castle, on the B9091 road between Croy and Clephanton, approximately 10 miles (16 kilometres) east of Inverness and the A9. The castle is administered by Ellel Ministries as a hotel and religious retreat. Access is available only with permission.

The Great Fraser Yew

O ne of Scotland's most remarkable yew trees (*Taxus baccata*) grows on the Knockie Estate, at Stratherrick, near Fort Augustus. Located on the wild shores of Loch Ness in a Site of Special Scientific Interest, the tree forms a grove of about 20 stems. Uniquely for yew, these have sprung up from root suckers which have collectively created a dense, spreading grove with a circumference of 110 metres (361 feet). The central, "mother" stem measures 4.58 metres (15 feet) in girth, at ground level. This ancient yew was traditionally the gathering point for the Clan Fraser in times of trouble. Its age is unknown, although it might be as old as 700 years.

The southern bank of Loch Ness on the Knockie Estate, near Fort Augustus, Highland. It is reached by a strenuous 4.8 kilometre (3 mile) walk across moorland. Access is available only by permission.

The Seer Oak

The Wester Ross village of Stromeferry has a very special sessile oak tree (*Quercus petraea*). The Brahan Seer, Coinneach (Kenneth) Odhar, prophesied in the late 17th century that it would be a very bad day for the people of the district if any two men could link arms around the trunk of the big oak tree. Thankfully, this has never been achieved. The oak stands out as the biggest in the area by far, and the trunk, measuring 4.62 metres (15 feet) in girth, is impossible for two men to encircle.

Alongside a small public road between the hamlets of Achmore and Braeintra, near the village of Stromeferry, Wester Ross, Highland. Public access is available.

Dughall Mor

Reelig Glen, south of the A862 near Beauly, about 11.3 kilometres (7 miles) west of Inverness, Highland. Turn off the A862 towards Moniack. The Glen is managed by Forestry Commission Scotland. Public access and car parking are available, and Dughall Mor is sign-posted on the forest walk.

The tallest tree so far recorded in the United Kingdom, and indeed Europe, is a Douglas fir (*Pseudotsuga menziesii*) in Reelig Glen, near Inverness. Planted as recently as 1882, this tall and elegant specimen has reached a staggering height of 64 metres (210 feet), when measured in 2005. Forestry Commission Scotland ran a competition among local people to find a name for this champion of the tree world, and have christened it Dughall Mor, which in Gaelic means "big dark stranger".

Dughall Mor forms part of a grove of very tall Douglas firs that comprise the largest concentration of trees exceeding 55 metres (180 feet) anywhere in the British Isles. They are so straight and tall that one was felled to provide a replacement mast for the Discovery, the ship in which explorer Sir Robert Scott sailed to the Antarctic. (The "Discovery" is now berthed at Dundee.) This fir is obviously thriving in the fertile and sheltered environment of the glen, with a ready supply of moisture from the Moniack Burn. This deceptive champion has a relatively slender trunk and its great height is difficult to appreciate, surrounded as it is by other giants.

Springtime in Reelig Glen, with a stand of massive Douglas firs visible through the beeches.

Duncan Forbes' Oak

A most unusual, pot-bellied oak stands isolated in a field overlooking the Beauly Firth west of Inverness. It takes its name from Duncan Forbes of Culloden (1685 - 1747), who was Lord President of the Court of Session during the second Jacobite uprising. He is said to have sat under this remarkable specimen to think and plan.

Loyal to the King, Forbes was the bane of the Jacobite cause and did much to oppose the rebels. Indeed, he was instrumental in the defeat of Bonnie Prince Charlie at the battle of Culloden (1746), and was subsequently credited as saving Scotland for the House of Hanover. Such was his power and influence at the time that he was known in the Highlands as "King Duncan". The "King" is dead, but the old oak tree lives on, forever associated with this historical figure.

It is notable for its grossly swollen and distended trunk, measuring 6.28 metres (20 feet 8 inches) in girth at its widest point. The reason for the swelling is a huge burr which exaggerates its girth. Repeated browsing by the resident flock of sheep might have stimulated this unusual form of growth. At only 5 metres (16 feet) in height, this living barrel of a tree has a healthy, flat-topped crown.

On private agricultural land west of Inverness, Highland.

Beauly Sycamore

This fine, open-grown sycamore (*Acer pseudoplatanus*) dominates the picturesque ruins of Beauly Priory, its dome-shaped canopy spreading over the weather-worn gravestones which lie scattered around its roots. The short, squat trunk measures 5.33 metres (17 feet 6 inches) in girth, and the robust framework of large limbs attains a height of 17.5 metres (57 feet 8 inches). Nothing is known of its age or origin, but it is clearly of considerable antiquity and has been a feature of the site for many centuries.

In addition to the sycamore, three ancient pollarded wych elms (*Ulmus glabra*) stand close by, their heavily decayed trunks sprouting fresh, healthy growth. The tree immediately next to the main gate has a particularly gnarled and burred trunk supporting branches of outlandish appearance. So far, these fine veterans have escaped the ravages of Dutch elm disease, and might possibly be some of the oldest surviving examples of their species in the United Kingdom.

Beauly Priory was founded in 1230 by monks of the Valliscaulian Order, under the patronage of Sir John Bisset. Mary, Queen of Scots, paid a visit to the abbey in 1564 en route to Dingwall, and was reportedly impressed with the beauty of the abbey and its orchard.

Beauly Priory stands at the east end of the main square in the town of Beauly, approximately 21 kilometres (13 miles) west of Inverness, Highland. It is managed by Historic Scotland, and there is free public access throughout the year. In the event of the main gate off the square being locked, there is usually a sign telling where the key is held.

The Fairburn Sitka

The grounds of Fairburn House, near Contin, Easter Ross, are home to many fine trees. The most impressive is the massive Sitka spruce (*Picea sitchensis*) which dominates the lawn. Its heavily branched trunk measures 7.83 metres (25 feet 8 inches) in girth, and is one of the largest recorded for this species in the

The grounds of Fairburn House, 3.2 kilometres (2 miles) south of Contin, Highland. The grounds are open to the public on a limited number of days each year. At other times access is available only with permission.

United Kingdom. Its height is equally impressive at 44.8 metres (147 feet). The healthy foliage extends down to ground level, an unusual feature on a species normally grown in dense plantations. The Fairburn tree was probably planted shortly after the introduction of Sitka spruce by David Douglas in 1832, and is now a superb specimen of great size and character.

The Brahan Elm

The largest-girthed wych elm (*Ulmus glabra*) in the United Kingdom resides at Brahan Estate, Easter Ross. Planted in 1735, this "champion" measures 7.03 metres (23 feet) in girth, reaching a height of 25.6 metres (84 feet) in 2002. It is a fine, open-grown specimen in an area of historic parkland, and still enjoys good health, despite its exposed location. Wych elm is native to the UK, and is the species of elm most commonly found in Scotland. The Brahan tree has so far escaped the ravages of Dutch elm disease, a fungus spread from tree to tree by a bark beetle.

Private parkland south of Brahan House, on Brahan estate, on the south side of the A835 road about 4.8 kilometres (3 miles) west of Maryburgh, Easter Ross, Highland. Access is available only by permission.

1550
Sweet Chestnut

The tree with the oldest recorded planting date in Scotland is the superb sweet chestnut (*Castanea sativa*) at Castle Leod, Strathpeffer. Estate records show that the tree was planted in 1550 by John Mackenzie (1480 - 1556), 9th Chief of Kintail and a Privy Councillor to King James V and Mary, Queen of Scots.

The tree is an outstanding specimen of very large size. The long, clean trunk measures 8.1 metres (26 feet 7 inches) in girth and the lofty canopy has attained a height of 28 metres (92 feet). Historical measurements of the trunk's girth suggest a relatively slow rate of growth. In 1867 the girth was 5.5 metres (18 feet 2 inches), in 1908 6.4 metres (21 feet 6 inches), and in 1938 7.1 metres (23 feet 3 inches). The thick, fissured bark on the bole displays a strong spiral twist, which is very characteristic of old sweet chestnuts. The angle of the spiral tends to increase as trees age, although the grain of the underlying timber normally remains vertical. Despite its very great age, the Castle Leod tree is in remarkably good health. Unfortunately, a second, smaller sweet chestnut also dating from 1550 was lost in a gale in 1979.

The grounds of Castle Leod, off the A834 road about 0.8 kilometres (half a mile) east of Strathpeffer, Easter Ross, Highland. The grounds are open to the public at certain times of the year.

The Castle Leod Redwood

The tallest giant redwood (*Sequoiadendron giganteum*) so far recorded in the United Kingdom stands in the grounds of Castle Leod, Strathpeffer. It measures a staggering 52 metres (170 feet) tall, and its equally impressive trunk has a girth of 8.9 metres (29 feet 3 inches). The tree is also notable as one of the few surviving original introductions of this species, brought to these shores by the Scottish botanist and plant collector, John Matthew, in 1853.

The estate records it as being planted in 1853 to commemorate the first birthday of Francis Mackenzie, Viscount Tarbat and later Earl of Cromartie. Regular measurements taken since 1891 show rapid growth.

By 1954, only 100 years after planting, the tree had already topped 30 metres (98 feet) and the beautifully flared trunk had attained a girth of 6.9 metres (22 feet 9 inches). The tree is a handsome and stately specimen, with a shapely, spire-like crown so typical of the species.

The giant redwood is often referred to as Wellingtonia, a name given to it by John Lindley of the Horticultural Society of London. He thought it appropriate that the world's most impressive tree should commemorate the Duke of Wellington, who had died the year before.

The champion giant redwood may be seen to the immediate right of the castle.

The grounds of Castle Leod, off the A834 0.8 kilometres
(half a mile) east of Strathpeffer, Easter Ross, Highland.
The grounds are open to the public at certain times of the year.

Champion Aspen

This fine specimen of aspen (*Populus tremula*) is the largest so far recorded for its species, and a UK champion.[1] The trunk measured 2.9 metres in girth (9 feet 6 inches) in 2006, and the lofty canopy has attained a height of 21 metres (69 feet). It is undoubtedly of exceptional size for a species whose slender trunks are normally of more modest proportions.

Aspen is a native species of poplar which is widely distributed throughout Scotland. It prefers cooler climes and is nowhere more at home than in the rugged Highlands, where it often grows side by side with Scots pine and birch. The tree's Latin name, *tremula*, is derived from the leaves, which tremble and shake in even the slightest of breezes. This fluttering habit means that trees almost seem to shimmer in the landscape. The rustling sound of the foliage is equally attractive, and this characteristic gave rise to the tree's more traditional name of "quaking aspen". The bright, butter-yellow shades of the autumn foliage is another of the tree's notable attributes.

Aspen, like most poplars, is not a long-lived species: individual trees seldom survive for more than a century before decay and senility set in. However, it has a remarkable and highly successful method of regeneration. Suckers emerge from the extensive root system, surrounding the "mother" tree in an ever-extending ring of clonal growth. In exceptional cases, suckers have been recorded up to 40 metres (131 feet) from the parent tree. A tree near Chepstow, in Wales, was recorded with more than 1000 individual stems, forming its own little copse covering a hectare (2.5 acres). The age of the root stock of such a tree could be centuries, if not thousands, of years old. [2]

3.5 miles (5.6 kilometres) west of the village of Ardgay, Sutherland, on an unclassified road on the south bank of the River Carron. The tree stands within a small copse next to a burn 10 metres back from the public road, between Wester Dounie Cottage and Gruinards Farm. It is readily viewed from the public road.

The Dundonnell Yew

This ancient and beautiful yew (*Taxus baccata*) forms the centrepiece of a private garden in Dundonnell, near Ullapool, Highland. It appears to have been coppiced many years ago, and the resulting re-growth has formed a ring of interlaced stems. Its huge trunk, one of the largest recorded for yew in Scotland, measures 7 metres (23 feet) in girth at ground level. Although there are no records of its age, the tree is certainly very old: estimates vary widely, between 600 and 2000 years. The tree is notable for another reason: it has achieved its great size despite growing at the unusually high latitude for yews of 57 degrees north.

The private garden of Dundonnell House, near Dundonnell, Wester Ross, Highland. Access is available only by permission, although the garden is also open on selected days through Scotland's Garden Scheme.

The Big Tree of Orkney

Orkney's biggest and oldest tree stands in Kirkwall's Main Street. A well known local landmark, this solitary sycamore (*Acer pseudoplatanus*) is known as The Big Tree, because Orkney's windswept environment means that few trees can survive or grow to any appreciable size. It appears to have arisen as a windblown seedling, and is now several centuries old. Urban development has encroached heavily on the tree, which is displaying symptoms of decline. Its hollow trunk has been heavily cut back to a stump of about 3 metres (10 feet). However, the tree is clearly a great survivor, and has sprouted new, healthy growth from the cut stump.

Main Street, Kirkwall, Orkney Islands. Public access is available.

References

In Memoriam – 19th Century (page 20)
1 Strutt J G: *Sylva Britannica 1830*, London. p132.
2 Strutt. p134.
3 Strutt. p151.

Heritage Tree Legacy (page 24)
1 Elwes H and Henry A: *The Trees of Great Britain & Ireland*. Edinburgh, 1906–13. p23.

The Drumlanrig Sycamore (page 32)
1 6th Earl of Haddington: *Forest Trees;: Some Directions about the Raising of Forest Trees*, c.1761. p21.

The Auld Yew Tree of Loudon (page 38)
1 Hutchison R: *On the Old and Remarkable Yew Trees in Scotland in Transactions of the Royal Arboricultural Society*, 1891. p379.

The 1725 Larches Larch (page 43)
1 *Principle Excursions of the Innerleithen Alpine Club during the Years 1889-94.*

King of the Woods (page 47)
1 Selby P J: *British Forest Trees*, 1842.
2 *Penny Magazine*, 1842. p47.

Hirsel Tulip (page 52)
1 Evelyn J: *Silva: or a Discourse of Forest Trees, and the Propagation of Timber in his Majesty's Dominions*. Royal Society, 15 October 1662. p73.
2 Loudon J C: *Arboretum et Fruticetum Britannicum or The Trees and Shrubs of Britain*. London, 1854. p284.
3 Loudon. p290.
4 Elwes H and Henry A: *The Trees of Great Britain & Ireland*. Edinburgh, 1906–13. p72.

Dryburgh Abbey (page 54)
1 Lowe J: *The Yew Trees of Britain and Northern Ireland*, 1897. p208.

The Collier's Oak (page 60)
1 Turnbull G: *A South Ayrshire Parish*, 1908. p121.

The Ormiston Yew (page 81)
1 Martine J: *Reminiscences and Notices of the Parishes of the County of Haddington*, 1890. p153.

The Whittingehame Yew (page 82)
1 Martine J: *Reminiscences and Notices of the Parishes of the County of Haddington*, 1890. p251.

Newbattle Abbey Sycamore (page 86)
1 Mitchell A: *Alan Mitchell's Trees of Britain*. Harper Collins, 1996. p184.

Dalkeith Park Oaks (page 87)
1 Rackham O: *Trees and Woodland in the British Landscape*, 1976. p142.

Stevenson's Yew (page 88)
1 Stevenson R L: 'To Minnie', in *A Child's Garden of Verses*, 1885.
2 Stevenson R L: 'The Manse', in *Memories and Portraits*, 1887.

Lady Miller's Beech (page 101)
1 Snoddy T G: *'Tween Forth and Tay*, 1966.

King James VI Sycamore (page 108)
1 Hunter T: *Woods, Forests and Estates of Perthshire*, 1883. p103.

The Scone Douglas Fir (page 112)
1 Elwes H and Henry A: *The Trees of Great Britain & Ireland*. Edinburgh, 1906–13. p83.

The King of the Forest (page 115)
1 Urquhart J D: *Historical Sketches of Scone*, 1883.

The Pepperwell Oak (page 116)
1 Hunter T: *Woods, Forests and Estates of Perthshire*, 1883. p125.

Mother and Father Douglas (page 117)

1 Mitchell A L and House S: *David Douglas: Explorer and Botanist*, 1999. p187.

The Parent Larch (page 135)

1 *Account of the larch plantation on the estates of Atholl and Dunkeld. Executed by the late John, Duke of Atholl.* Perth, 1832.
2 Mitchell A: *Alan Mitchell's Trees of Britain*, 1996. p73.

The Monzie Larch (page 138)

1 Mitchell A: *Alan Mitchell's Trees of Britain*, 1996. p73.
2 *Highland and Agricultural Society of Scotland Old and Remarkable Trees in Scotland*, 1867. p70.

The Fortingall Yew (page 149)

1 *Philosophical Transactions of the Royal Society.* Vol 59, Dec 1769. p23.
2 Neil, Dr: *Edinburgh Philosophical Journal*, 1833.
3 Loudon J C: *Arboretum et Fruticetum Britannicum or The Trees and Shrubs of Britain.* London, 1854. p2079.

Madroña at Castle Menzies (page 152)

1 Scott A: *A Pleasure in Scottish Trees*, 2002. p153.

Kenmore Coast Redwoods (page 153)

1 Van Pelt R: *Forest Giants of the Pacific Coast*, 2001. p17.

The Clachan Oak (page 182)

1 Highland and Agricultural Society of Scotland: *Old and Remarkable Trees in Scotland*, 1867. p177.

The Great Yew at Broich (page 187)

1 Highland and Agricultural Society of Scotland: *Old and Remarkable Trees in Scotland*, 1867. p227.
2 Hutchison R: *On the Old and Remarkable Yew Trees in Scotland in Transactions of the Royal Arboricultural Society*, 1891. p403.

Inchmahome Veterans (page 188)

1 Hunter T: *Woods, Forests and Estates of Perthshire*, 1883. p311.

Robert the Bruce's Yew (page 193)

1 Danielewski J: *Loch Lomond in Old Picture Postcards*, 1987.

The Mightiest Conifer in Europe (page 195)

1 Evelyn J: *Silva: or a Discourse of Forest Trees, and the Propagation of Timber in his Majesty's Dominions.* Royal Society, 15 October 1662.
2 *Transactions of the Scottish Arboricultural Society. Volume IX:* p174.
3 Elwes H and Henry A: *The Trees of Great Britain & Ireland.* Edinburgh, 1906-13. p730.

The Ardkinglas Grand Fir (page 196)

1 Tree Register of the British Isles, 2002.

Darnaway Oak (page 222)

1 Phillips M T T: *The History of the Ancient Oak Forest of Darnaway and its Timber.* Scottish Forestry 55(3), 2001. p159.
2 Anon: *The Royal Scottish Arboricultural Society 4th Annual Excursion*, 1881.
3 Grigor J: *Arboriculture, or a Practical Treatise on Raising and Managing Forest Trees*, 1881. p270.

The Kilravock Castle Layering Beech (page 227)

1 Miles A: *Silva.* Ebury Press, 1999.

The Champion Aspen (page 242)

1 Johnson O (ed.) – *Champion Trees of Britain and Ireland.* Whittet Books, 2003. p81.
2 More D and White J – *Trees of Britain and Northern Europe.* Cassel, 2003. p265.

Noteworthy Scottish Tree Collection Websites

www.rbge.org.uk

National botanic gardens: Benmore Botanic Garden, Dawyck Botanic Garden, Logan Botanic Garden, Royal Botanic Garden Edinburgh.

www.gardens-of-argyll.co.uk

Argyll Garden collections, including: Achamore, Ardchattan Priory, Ardkinglas, Ardtornish, Arduaine, Crarae, Kilmory Woodland Park, Stonefield Castle Hotel and Garden, and Torosay Castle and Garden.

www.nts.org.uk

National Trust collections, including: Crathes, Falkland, Inverewe Garden.

www.gardensofscotland.org

National gardens, including: Acnacloich, Bolfracks, Corsock House, Floors Castle, Kildrummy, Monteviot, Scone Palace, and Wemyss Castle.

www.gardenvisit.com

National gardens, including: Cawdor Castle, Crathes Castle, Drummond Castle, Glendoik.

www.gardenhistory.org.uk

National database of gardens, including: Blair Castle, Glasgow Botanic gardens.

www.st-andrews.ac.uk/~gdk/stabotanic/links.htm

Botanic gardens including Cruikshank Botanic Garden Aberdeen, Dundee Botanic Garden.

www.greatbritishgardens.co.uk

www.ancient-trees.org.uk

Ancient Tree Forum

www.tree-register.org

Tree Register of The British Isles

Index

Map references are given in brackets.

continued overleaf...

The Tree Council – working together for trees

Conservation charity The Tree Council, the United Kingdom's leading tree campaigning partnership, is dedicated to inspiring, initiating and enabling effective action for trees in town and countryside. It campaigns to make more people aware that trees matter – and that effective action for trees and woods means a great deal more than just planting new ones. It also works towards more trees, of the right kind and in the right place, and better care for all trees, of all ages.

The Tree Council grew out of 1973's National Tree Year, with its slogan of "Plant a Tree in '73". It was founded the following year as an umbrella body for organisations working together for trees – planting, caring for and enjoying them – and as a forum for tackling issues relating to trees and woods. Members range from professional, non-government, specialist and trade organisations, including other conservation charities, to local authorities and government agencies.

Every year the Tree Council organises a series of UK-wide festivals to celebrate trees, with events planned by its members, its volunteer Tree Wardens, and other supporters. The calendar begins with Seed Gathering Season which starts on the autumn equinox and runs for a month, followed by National Tree Week at the end of November to launch the planting season, The Tree Care Campaign launched on the third weekend in March, and Walk in the Woods in May. For further information visit www.treecouncil.org.uk

Forestry Commission Scotland

Forestry Commission Scotland is part of the Forestry Commission, which is the government department for forestry in Great Britain. It serves as the forestry department of the Scottish Executive (the government of Scotland) by advising on and implementing forestry policy in Scotland. Its mission is to protect and expand Scotland's forests and woodlands and increase their value to society and the environment.

Forestry Commission Scotland manages more than 660,000 hectares of national forests and other land to provide a wide range of public benefits, including sustainable timber production, public recreation, environmental protection, and rural and community development. It supports other woodland owners by providing: grants to plant, regenerate, manage and improve woodland; licences to fell trees; and advice and regulation.

It is directed by Scottish Ministers through a Great Britain Board of Forestry Commissioners and a National Committee for Scotland, and is funded by the Scottish Parliament. It works closely with the Scottish Executive, particularly its Environment & Rural Affairs Department, to implement the Scottish Forestry Strategy, which is closely integrated with other aspects of land use and economic policy. It also contributes to many other aspects of wider Scottish Executive policy, such as the environment, health, education, rural transport, tourism, and improving lives in deprived areas of Scotland's towns and cities.

For further information, visit www.forestry.gov.uk/scotland telephone 0845 FORESTS (0845 367 3787); or e-mail enquiries@forestry.gsi.gov.uk

Archie Miles

A professional photographer for more than thirty years, and a writer for about fifteen years, he has worked in the industrial, tourism and environmental sectors, travelling worldwide, but always had an abiding passion for landscape and natural history. A specialisation over the last twelve years has seen him carving a distinctive niche in the world of trees, and he works on a regular basis with both the Tree Council and the Woodland Trust. He has travelled the length and breadth of the British Isles to photograph many of the country's greatest and rarest trees as well as a huge diversity of woodland types. He runs a successful picture library and a postcard publishing business. The picture library now contains one of the most comprehensive collections of British tree photographs in the country – over 300,000 images!

His best-selling book, *Silva – The Tree in Britain* (Ebury Press – 1999), has sold in excess of 20,000 copies, he was part of the team that produced *The Heritage Trees of Britain and Northern Ireland* (Constable/The Tree Council – 2004), and has just completed a tie-in book for a new BBC 2 series – *The Trees that made Britain*.

He lives with his family and assorted animals in Herefordshire. www.archiemiles.co.uk

Edward Parker

Edward Parker is a well-known photographer and writer who specialises in environmental and social issues around the world. He is particularly renowned for his photography of ancient trees and rainforests.

His work has taken him to more than 40 countries and he has worked for many years with organizations that include the World Wide Fund for Nature (WWF-UK), World Wildlife Fund International (WWF-International), the Tropical Forest Trust, the Tree Council and the Forest Stewardship Council.

Edward Parker has written or co-written more than 30 books including *Ancient Trees – Trees That Live for a Thousand Years*, which he photographed and co-wrote. More recently he was the photographer for *Plants For People* and *Out of Eden* – two major books published for the Eden Project. He has twice been "highly commended" in the Wildlife Photographer of the Year competition and was short-listed for Environmental Photojournalist of the year in 2002 at the British Environment and Media Awards. www.edwardparker.com

Donald Rodger

Donald Rodger is an independent arboricultural consultant based in East Lothian. He provides specialist advice on the care and management of amenity trees to a broad range of public and private sector clients throughout Scotland. He has a particular interest in heritage trees and has spent many years researching and recording them. He is a Chartered Forester, a Chartered Biologist and a Fellow and Registered Consultant of the Arboricultural Association. www.donaldrodger.co.uk

Acknowledgements

The authors would like to record their thanks to the owners and custodians of the various trees for their willing assistance in providing access and information, without which this book could not have been produced. We are also indebted to the many Tree Wardens and members of the public who brought some of the lesser known trees to our attention.

In particular, thanks are extended to James McDougall of the Forestry Commission for his painstaking research into tree ownership and undertaking valuable administrative work behind the scenes. We are also grateful to John Miller and Michael Smith, Tree Consultants, for their help with this project.

Thanks are extended to the Tree Register of the British Isles and the many friends and colleagues throughout Scotland who have provided valuable information on many of the trees.

Thanks are also extended to George MacMillan of Finlaystone House – who did his utmost to locate archive pictures of the moving of the yew tree in 1900, and to the Edinburgh School of Music for kind permission to photograph the Corstorphine Violin. We are also indebted to Steve Cole of the Forestry Commission for his work on the maps, to Jacky Ferneyhough (Pen Dragon) for indexing and to Simon Mayoh and Geoff Carter of Carter Graphics for their work on the book's design.

Photographs Copyright ©

Archie Miles: Cover and pp. 1,2,8,10,12,13,14,15,17,19,20,21,23,24,25,27,30,32,33,34,37,38-9,44,45, 50,53,54,55,56,57,58,59,60,61,62,63,64,65,67,71,73,76,80,83,84,85(top),90,93,94,95,98,99,100,101,103, 107,108,109,113,114,115,117,119,129,130,134,136,137,138,139,142,145,148,154,155,156,160,161,163, 164,165,167,169,170,171,174,175,177,178,179,180,185,188,189,190,201,203,211,216,217,218,219,220, 222,223,226,231,236,237,238,240,241,242,244

Edward Parker: pp. 11,22,40,42,43,46,47,49,66,68,69,70,79,86,87,89,96,97,104,106,110,116,121,122, 124,125,127,128,132,133,141,143,144,146,147,150,151,152,153,173,183,186,192,194,197,199,200,204, 205,207,213,214,221,224,229,230,233,234,243

Donald Rodger: pp. 85(bottom),105

Jon Stokes Collection: pp. 36,78,112,135,140,149

Andy McGeeney: p228

Orkney Photographic: p245

The Linnean Society, London: p210

The Tim Winter Postcard Collection: pp. 102,118,123,131,182,190(inset),193

Courtesy Felix Dennis Collection: pp. 15,82

Courtesy Mr and Mrs J Linsley: pp. 81(inset),88

Courtesy George MacMillan (Finlaystone House) and Lloyd Smith: p172

Maps designed by Simon Mayoh